Catholics Awake!
Marino Restrepo

Pilgrims of Love Foundation

Foreword

Throughout history, the Catholic Church has been profoundly united to what we might call the 'cycles' of humanity. But, rather than mirroring this humanity exactly, the Church's primary purpose, in each of these cycles has been to reflect God. In the cycle in which we are presently living, we witness the sad phenomenon of a Catholic Church which reflects more the influence of the world than that of the Spirit of God.

As the title suggests, this book is intended as a wake-up call for *The People of God*. It explores how and why clergy, religious and laity are largely failing in the solemn mission entrusted to them by the Lord Jesus, an evangelizing mission which is, at once, the primary task and the very *raison d'être* of the Church. Compelled by a deep love for the Lord and His Church, the author's critique seeks not to judge or condemn but to open people's eyes, minds and hearts to the magnificence and the enormity of the responsibility enjoined on them by their baptismal vocation, which is the very lifeblood of prophetic ministry.

This book, then, seeks to help every Catholic to grow stronger and more keenly aware of the spiritual battle that rages around us, so that we might better defend our spiritual territories and win more souls for God's Kingdom.

Content

Introduction i

The True Catholic 1

Spiritual Armor 5

Preparation for the Battle 9

Spiritual Nourishment 13

The Way, the Truth and the Life 19

Assimilating the Truth 23

Preparation to Serve 27

God's Invisible Power 33

The Weapons of Faith 37

Response to a Weakened Church 43

The Spiritual Battle 51

The Seduction of the Devil 59

Awakening the Church 67

Resisting the Forces of Evil 75

A Simple Choice 81

The Authority of the People of God 87

The Ecclesiastical Hierarchy 91

Guardian of the Truth 99

The Enemy Within 103

The Limitations of Reason 107

Life After Life 113

Obedience 117

The Sacramental Economy 121

Baptism 125

Penance and Reconciliation: Confession 131

The Eucharist: Holy Communion 137

Confirmation 143

Holy Orders 153

Holy Matrimony 169

The Sacramentals 177

The Catholic Funeral 181

The Vocation of Man: Life in the Spirit 185

The Nature of Sin 189

Virtues 195

Spiritual Growth 199

Prayer 201

Interior Silence 209

Modern Theologies 219

The Profession of Faith 223

Conclusion 231

In Homage to the Catholic Church

Introduction

We urgently need to change the way we live our faith. Many Catholics have fallen prey to the spirit of the world, weakening the Church to such a degree that many Catholics are now struggling to hold on to the Faith. Grave sin has penetrated the very heart of priestly and religious life. Many of the traditional Religious Orders have gradually disappeared, failing to attract new vocations and to inspire young people. On the many missionary journeys I have undertaken for the Catholic Church, spanning five continents over fifteen years, I have seen many convents, monasteries and churches being closed and turned into exclusive, commercial premises and galleries to showcase religious art. I have even known churches to be acquired by unscrupulous building developers to be used as nightclubs and bars. Some keep the religious art that was formerly part of the sacred and religious life of the Church so that now we have holy images forming the backdrop to a nightlife of sin and debauchery.

It is absolutely vital that we do all we can to preserve our Catholic identity and try to rediscover the true nature of our Catholic mission. We need to realize that our Catholic heritage is an unimaginable gift which we have a serious responsibility to safeguard and share with all humanity. We cannot allow our places of worship to be turned into museums and dens of iniquity. We must never lose sight of our Catholic culture or become complacent towards the great spiritual wealth of our Sacred Tradition with its images, iconography and holy relics.

Recently I visited some antique stores, because I discovered that many sacred objects are regularly being removed from churches and sold at premium prices to unprincipled antique dealers. These items are taken from convents and monasteries, and even from churches and parishes that may have adopted New Age practices, Marxist philosophies, heresies or simply Modernism. In antique stores nowadays, it is quite common to find relics, chalices, ciboria, patens, monstrances and liturgical vestments - the list is endless. Sadly, those who supply these sacred objects are priests, Catholic men and women or religious, all seduced by avarice.

The Church calls this practice the sin of simony after Simon the Magician who wanted to use God's powers to win fame and money (Acts. 8:18-24). Those who sell sacred objects of the Church fall into this sin. What is most terrible about the sale of these sacred objects is the sacrilegious use to which they are ultimately employed, something too shocking for me to want to address in these lines.

With regard to immorality and disobedience, we are living through one of the greatest crises of modern times. Although it is true that there will always be a faithful remnant of priests, religious and laity in the Catholic Church, that is to say, those who are holy and committed in the true sense of the word, we cannot forget that this immorality and disobedience has seized hold of vast numbers of the clergy and religious.

To address the question of what to do in the face of these problems is one of the reasons for my writing this book. In examining these sad facts, it must be acknowledged that those Catholics - priests, religious and laity - who are active and mired in grave sin in the Church today, are themselves the products of 'modern-day' Catholic families.

If we are even to begin to address the root cause of the problems in the Church today, we must start by examining our modern Catholic society which has become so contaminated that it no longer can be said to belong to God. The sad truth is that the Catholic family of today has been largely corrupted at its heart by the worldly spirit of decadence. These damaged, dysfunctional and broken Catholic families beget damaged, dysfunctional and broken individual Catholics who, in turn beget a damaged, dysfunctional and broken Catholic Church. This is why the call to the *New Evangelization*, of which we speak today in our Catholic Church, is not just for Europe as initially intended. We must begin by evangelizing Catholic families the world over because the Catholic family is the womb of the Lord's Church and the seedbed of all vocations.

First, Jesus called his disciples and then he sent them out (Luke 9: 1-6). We are all numbered among those the Lord sends out, as long as we desire to wake up to the seriousness of this responsibility and to earnestly seek to fulfill our duty as children of God and members of His Church.

The True Catholic

It is vital that our relationship with God be defined on a clear understanding that He is God and we are His creatures (Exod. 3:13-15). Only in this way shall we be able to submit to Him in humility and meekness of heart.

As Christians, our religion is the means by which we encounter the spiritual world. Although, generally, we are accepting of our religion, we are not as fully and unconditionally accepting of God. This creates an inner conflict for the Christian; one with which he will wrestle throughout his entire life, as he constantly vacillates between being 'of God', on the one hand, and being 'of himself and the world' on the other.

A useful way to think about the life-long journey of conversion is as one in which we are to ceaselessly strive for the straight way to God; seeking to die to ourselves and to surrender entirely to God's lordship in all things.

I have been a lay missionary for the past fifteen years. My return to the Catholic Church took place almost two years before I became a missionary. Some sixteen years have now passed since I was rescued by Our Lord Jesus Christ from the most profound darkness in which I lived, or, should I say, in which I was spiritually dead, for thirty-three years.

During these years of mission, in more than ninety countries worldwide, I felt the great need to exhort fellow Catholics to acquire a more profound awareness of the Faith, a greater clarity and conception of the Church, her transcendental nature and mystical identity as the 'People of God'. My desire, however, did not come from some sense of superior knowledge or virtue, but quite the reverse. What impelled me was the responsibility I felt for having inflicted on the Church so many of the evils which I describe in these pages.

True change always begins at home, with oneself. So, when I point out the evil that is in the Church and in the world, I know, at the same time, that I am also pointing the finger squarely at myself.

When I came back to the Church, I was really dismayed by the huge number of scandals caused by unfaithful priests and religious, with their secret homosexual lives, pedophilia and various other sordid depravities, too shameful even to mention. I was perplexed by the widespread acceptance by so many religious of various pagan teachings and philosophies, including: yoga; the enneagram; alternative medicine; mind control techniques, magic and all sorts of superstitions; heretical beliefs and Marxist ideologies. The list seemed endless.

What is one to do in the face of such ubiquitous evil? We know that it is no longer an option to remain silent and passive, but is it even possible for us to make a difference? Is there any hope at all?

One of the main reasons there is so much indifference towards what is happening in the Church is because we simply no longer know who we really are. We are unaware of the power that Our Lord Jesus has given us.

If we are to summon the courage that we need to confront Satan and free ourselves from the apathy and the paralyzing fear gripping us, we must first confront ourselves by asking a fundamental and far-reaching question - are we prepared to give our life for God's Church?

There are parishes in many parts of the world today where priests commit such monstrous sacrileges that they can no longer even be said to be Catholic. They have become true sons of darkness who do immense harm to the flocks entrusted to them, leading many with them into the darkness. These congregations can no longer even hear the truth without it arousing in them feelings of anger and despair.

In some of these parishes, I found that the mere mention of certain realities such as hell, or describing the forces of evil as actual spiritual beings, or just reminding people about sin and the need for the sacrament of Confession, so enraged people that I often came close to being physically attacked.

Such experiences bring to mind Saint Paul's words when he wrote:

> For the time is coming when people will not endure sound teaching but... will accumulate for themselves teachers to suit their own likings. (2 Tim. 4:3-5)

Being a true Catholic means being conscious of the mission that God entrusted to us at Baptism which is to witness to His Kingdom and to proclaim His Word with the testimony of our life.

We must not fear the Evil One as we give witness to the truth before those who do not know it, or who simply choose to ignore it. There is hope, yes. There is a remedy, but first we must begin close to home by making changes in our own little lives. Then, the Holy Spirit will come to accompany us in our mission to save souls.

Indeed, there is hope, but everything depends on us - on our sincere conversion, on our awakening to a true Christian life and on our daring to give our lives for the Lord, and for His Church.

Spiritual Armor

As Christians, it is important for us to realize just what it is we are witnessing in today's civilization. In our globalized world, we see a humanity which, considering itself independent of God, looks to obtain everything, solely by human means. This 'Tower of Babel' phenomenon is readily observable in cities across the world. In fact, we can think of it as innate human behavior, imprinted in our very nature.

There is no doubt that the world has fabricated a counterfeit Christ and a counterfeit Christianity. There is so much talk of Christ today and such little evidence of Him in people's hearts. It is important that we know how to tell the difference. Being genuinely 'of Christ' means being crucified with him, being dead to sin, and to oneself. It means giving one's whole life to God. Being genuinely Christian means being genuinely like Christ and conformed completely to him.

From the moment of our Baptism, we are crucified mystically with Him. When we received our First Holy Communion, we began to be nourished with His Holy Body and Blood which strengthened the supernatural life which He first gave us at Baptism. At Confirmation, through the imposition of the bishop's hands, we received His Holy Spirit in an extraordinary way and were sent out by His Church to fulfill our mission;

an evangelizing mission to bear witness and to be beacons of hope and salvation for the many souls He would put in our path throughout our life. At the end of this earthly life, it is these souls for whom we will be called to account before the tribunal of the Lord.

Every true Christian is a little David coming forth to do battle with the giants of hell, armed only with the slingshot of his faith and with Christ, who is his rock. With these weapons, he will contend with the powers of the *Infernal Goliath*, the fallen spirits that live in eternity, outside of time and space. His battlefield is the invisible kingdom of the spiritual world.

Although we may join the battle in the material world, the battle is, in reality, a spiritual one relating, as it does, strictly and directly, to the eternal salvation of all humanity. We read of this in Saint Paul's Letter to the Ephesians, when he writes:

> Our battle is not against human forces, but against the rulers and authorities and their dark powers, that govern this world. We are struggling against the spirits and supernatural forces of evil. (Eph. 6:12)

The Catholic Church on earth is, in fact, one of a trinity of Churches; the *Church Triumphant* in Heaven, the *Church Suffering* in Purgatory and the *Church Militant* on Earth. The three form one body, or one army, known collectively as the *Communion of Saints*. They fight together for a single, common objective - the salvation of souls.

A Catholic must clearly understand three things if he is to be an effective soldier in this *Army of the Lord:* the mission that God has entrusted to him; the immensity of his task; and the power of his Church. Otherwise, he is merely sleepwalking through the battle and will surely perish in his slumber.

It is not by chance that we are born Catholic. It is by the grace of God. In the sacrament of Baptism this grace exorcizes us from the influence of evil, sets us free from original sin and unchains us from spiritual ancestral bondage.

Remaining faithful to Sacred Tradition sets Catholics in a state of obedience, and unites them to the mystical Body of Christ, which is the Church. In this position, or state, we are safeguarded against enemy attacks and preserved in unity and freedom.

The forces of darkness have always, and will always, try to divide the Lord's Church. We see throughout our sacred history the devastating divisions wrought by this evil down through the ages. Some of these divisions will last, perhaps, until the end of time.

Jesus's circumcision was clear on God's plan, so being circumcised follow His submission and obedience to His earthly parents decisions. In His words, too, the Lord emphasized its importance when he said:

> Think not that I have come to abolish the law and the prophets; I have come not to abolish them but to fulfill them. (Matt. 5:17)

Fulfilling the Law and the Prophets, in this case, would mean abolishing the circumcision of the flesh and replacing it with the circumcision of the heart - something which came about with the consummation of Jesus' Passion. As we see in the example of His circumcision, however, and throughout his earthly life, Jesus subjected himself entirely to Judaic tradition.

Preparation for the Battle

If we are to become effective agents of God's Kingdom, we must first recognize ourselves as the children of God who have been called to active service in the Church, or the *Church Militant* to be more precise.

The spiritual battle, which we are called to join, demands discipline and rigorous training. Our preparation begins with an initial instruction in the Faith, where we acquire a basic knowledge of God and His precepts. However, as we grow and learn, by God's grace, we appropriate a more solid, spiritual understanding of the profound mysteries which have been revealed to us through *Sacred Scripture* and *Sacred Tradition*. This body of saving truth, which we call *the Deposit of The Faith,* was shaped and forged in the furnace of adversity, as the Church battled throughout the ages against the powers of darkness. It was refined, strengthened and purified by the blood of those martyrs who gave their own lifeblood, in union with the Precious Blood of the Savior, to be the very lifeblood of the Church and the seed of Christians. Their sacrifice continues to propel the Church on her unwavering pilgrimage, under the constant guidance of the Holy Spirit, to the *parousia,* that time when the Lord will come again.

Frequent reception of the sacraments of Confession and Holy Communion are absolutely vital if we are to fulfill our duty properly and rise to meet the challenge of battle. Only if we are faithful to God and continually strengthened by the sacraments and a life of deep prayer, can we possibly hope to overcome evil.

Of course, our struggle with evil is often an interior one. In these moments, we do have the graces of the Holy Spirit to help us, but these graces are somehow only fully available to us when we are fighting with all our might against our weaknesses and imperfections and striving ceaselessly to overcome our innate tendency to sin. Our Heavenly Father is perfectly just and merciful and when He sees our brave efforts, He looks upon us with great love and blesses us. We are assured that, through His Church, He will give us everything we need to defend ourselves from the snares of the enemy.

It is important to understand that to confront evil and to fight effectively against the forces that seek to hamper our progress towards God, we must be careful not to slip into easy compromises with sin. Because of our frail human nature, we readily fall into Satan's traps. But there is a remedy; there is a secret to overcoming this evil. When we humble ourselves, and lovingly resign ourselves to our falls, hastening to pick ourselves up and return to God, and if we do this without guilt or fear, but with sincere repentance, expressed perfectly through the sacrament of Confession, then we can be sure we are fully reconciled with God and our friendship with Him is restored.

When we live in complete fidelity to God, we are attentive to His call. His Holy Will becomes perfectly apparent to us. He is with us in the midst of our trials and sustains us with His grace. As He reminds Saint Paul, His grace is sufficient for us and is, "made perfect in weakness" (2 Cor. 12:9). This is precious knowledge which we must take to heart. It is Divine

Truth which we must allow to germinate in the core of our being. The Lord is infinite mercy. The mere fact of detesting the evil that is in us and rejecting it outright, will, by the grace of His Mercy, strengthen us, because He knows that we have not fully consented to that sin.

Life in obedience to God fills us with a light that blinds the enemy. The weak become strong in God and those who are faithful despite their weaknesses, are made strong and able to defeat the enemy of their souls. God strengthens His people in every battle, at every moment and in every situation. Even the most terrifying hoards of evil are easily brushed aside by the powerful hand of the Almighty, who will never abandon His faithful people.

Saint Augustine teaches that our true roots are in God and not in the world. We are not, therefore, subject to the law of spiritual gravity that tends to anchor us in the material plane. Planted above, we derive our nourishment, through the Holy Spirit, from the sap that we draw from the roots which we sink deep into the heart of God.

Spiritual Nourishment

In his letter to the Corinthians, Saint Paul draws a sharp distinction between the different stages of spiritual development. He writes:

> But I, brethren, could not address you as spiritual men, but as men of the flesh, as babes in Christ. I fed you with milk, not solid food; for you were not ready for it; and even yet you are not ready, for you are still of the flesh. For while there is jealousy and strife among you, are you not of the flesh and behaving like ordinary men? (1 Cor. 3:1-3).

What, in fact, does Saint Paul mean when he speaks about 'solid food'? And when, exactly, do we become those spiritual adults, ready for more substantial nourishment?

In Baptism, the Catholic is crucified with Christ. He dies to the flesh and the things of the flesh, receiving in his soul, through the anointing of the Holy Spirit, the gift of sanctifying grace. He becomes an adopted child of God and is endowed with supernatural life which elevates him above the natural endowments of human nature. In other words, he becomes more than the 'ordinary man' to whom Saint Paul refers. He is conformed fully to Christ and called to a life of complete obedience and abandonment to God, something which is not the case for adherents to pagan philosophies, belief systems and religions that do not come from God. The answer is the Eucharist. The baptized Catholic is, essentially, a Eucharistic vessel, and the Eucharist, the solid, spiritual sustenance of the spiritual adult.

Although Jesus walked a good distance with them on the road to Emmaus, it was only at 'the breaking of the bread' that the disciples were finally able to recognize him (Luke. 24:28-32).

This event marks the first occasion on which the truth of the doctrine of Jesus' *Real Presence* in the bread and wine is revealed to us. The one who denies that Jesus is truly alive and present in the Eucharist, even if he be a baptized Catholic, is denying Christ. He cannot, then, consume the solid spiritual food of God because he is unable to recognize Jesus and, as a consequence, lacks the basic awareness and predisposition one must have in order to receive Our Eucharistic Lord.

Having been nourished on spiritual milk alone, many Christians will face Jesus, the Supreme Judge, without the strength they need to fly straight to heaven. By the grace of God, such souls may attain salvation, but they will have to undergo a period of intense purification in Purgatory before they are able to enter into the fullness of God's glory. Again, Saint Paul describes this plainly in his letter to the Corinthians:

> Each man's work will become manifest; for the Day [of Judgment] will disclose it, because it will be revealed with fire, and the fire will test what sort of work each one has done. If the work which any man has built on the foundation survives, he will receive a reward. If any man's work is burned up, he will suffer loss, though he himself will be saved, but only through fire. (1 Cor. 3:13-15)

Solid spiritual food is a great grace that comes only from God. By means of this grace, God provides all the strength we might need to withstand even the fiercest spiritual onslaughts. But, before he can receive this solid food, the Christian must make a commitment of unconditional fidelity to God. This total consecration, this unwavering allegiance, is what is meant by the path of holiness. To go from being fed with milk to being nourished with solid food is, spiritually speaking, just like developing from adolescence into adulthood. It is very easy to identify a Catholic who is not receiving solid food. His behavior and attitudes are weak in facing the trials of life and he is unable to defend the Faith.

God is constantly calling us to have a strong faith and this requires a true conversion of heart. Only by arming ourselves with such a faith will we be able to fight the good fight of the Gospel. The ranks of the enemy are amassed at the gate. They look to exploit the weaknesses in our defenses and will take full advantage of each and every opportunity we give them in their efforts to devour us (1 Pet. 5:8).

Today, we are witnessing the last battle. It is a great war in which Good and Evil contend for those embodied souls on earth who are still journeying in exile. The Catholic who is well-armed has nothing to fear. He is perfectly capable of defending himself, his life and his mission, in faithfulness to God. Strengthened by the Eucharist, he receives a high degree of spiritual vitality. The Holy Spirit will use him where the fighting is most intense. The more we pay attention strategically in our daily life, the more missions the Holy Spirit assigns us. Our life starts to bear fruit in abundance and our serenity and confidence will intimidate any enemy who might dare to stand against us. We will be able to give peace and hope to the weak, bless the whole Militant Church and give great joy to the holy angels and the entire heavenly Court.

In these times, the Catholic is called to be more faithful than ever. People in general, now, are thirsting for God - even if they do not know it. They are looking for something they cannot describe or explain. This is because, as the human family, we are approaching the end times. Every soul on earth, regardless of race, nationality, cultural or religious persuasion, feels a great interior void that must be filled. Evil pretends to fill this void by disguising itself as true light. This is precisely why Jesus warned us about these times and the many false prophets that would appear, spreading all sorts of errors to deceive the people. (Matt. 24:3-14)

There are two kinds of human beings: those with a spiritual sense of life and those who are purely rational and materialistic. The spiritual group can have many categories, and encompasses all types of spiritual practices. Being spiritual does not necessarily mean knowing the Holy Spirit, however. The fact that a person has spiritual inclinations already makes him receptive to the spiritual world, a world that encompasses the states of good and evil.

Today, as never before, we witness a vast diversity of spiritual practices. Every conceivable philosophy, ideology, theosophy, esotericism, pagan belief system and atheistic, humanist science and every form of divination, sorcery, occult and a wide variety of satanic treatises and practices that come straight from hell, are readily accessible by a variety of means, all across the world.

The Catholic Church is the custodian of the sanctifying grace given to her by Christ. We are the people of God, a people that has been chosen to defend souls against the devil. Any attempt to engage the enemy under any other flag renders such combatants devastatingly vulnerable to diabolical attack. Unlike the Catholic Church, these simply do not possess the necessary spiritual authority required to battle effectively against the powers of darkness. The Lord gave this authority to the Church alone, in the person of Saint Peter, the first Pope, when he declared:

> I will give you the keys of the kingdom of heaven, and whatever you bind on earth shall be bound in heaven, and whatever you unbind on earth shall be unbound in heaven. (Matt. 16:19)

Strict obedience to the hierarchy of the Church is essential for the children of God. The greatest test of the genuineness of any Catholic is his ability to obey the ecclesiastical hierarchy, despite the fact that this hierarchy may often reflect the limitations and failures that we see manifested in the apostles themselves. We see, for example, that long after Jesus' ascension and the descent of the Paraclete, Saint Paul must reproach Saint Peter for being ashamed of the Gentile believers in front of James' Jewish friends when they came to visit him from Jerusalem (Gal. 2:11-21). This example, along with many others, serves to remind us that we need to be conscious that, ultimately, it is God we are serving and not men - even though we serve Him in the Church through human beings. We must rise above our humanity to overcome the obstructions we can become to one another because of our flawed humanity. We must be prepared to obey, unquestioningly, all that Holy Mother Church demands of us, primarily through Papal authority. Passing this test is crucial because it provides the faithful believer with a great deal of strength. God's graces flow freely through him making him an effective soldier in the battle against evil. In order to succeed, however, he must also be rooted in humility. This humility is the greatest of the weapons God gave to Saint Michael the Archangel to defeat Satan and all his rebel angels.

Another vital test that we need to pass relates directly to the First Commandment. We must put God first in everything and be absolutely dedicated to Him. We must live only for Him and consecrate all aspects of our life to His glory, rather than our own. We must submit completely to the will of God in all the events of our life. We need to realize that the way of holiness is achieved through a simple daily life of fidelity to God's commandments and to the Gospel of Christ Jesus, the Lord.

It is worth reflecting on this further by reading the *Catechism of the Catholic Church*, paragraphs 2084 - 2094.

The Way, the Truth and the Life

Christ's call seeks to awaken in His People the desire to live in the truth; to become aware that He alone is the Truth. We must look to God for the enlightening grace we need to help us grasp that He alone is the true Way. Only then can we come to understand, in the depths of our hearts, that Jesus is Life itself. Only by accepting Jesus as the Way, the Truth and the Life can the Christian live completely - spiritually and materially - in union with the Will of God.

This true vision of the Faith gives us wisdom in our relationship with God. It gives us a docility of heart and enables the gifts of the Holy Spirit to flow freely in us. It also gives us freedom in our relationships with those around us, as well as with those in authority. Such an awareness disposes the Christian to unconditional, life-long service of Jesus, his King and his Lord.

Nothing is more edifying for those seeking the truth than to encounter a Christian whose eyes shine with the light of unconditional obedience to God. The Gospel tells us: "No servant can serve two masters" (Luke 16:13). Because they truly serve God, such people are not 'of the world'. We may spend our entire life serving in the Church, living ostensibly pious lives and engaging in great works of charity, but if we do not get rid of everything in our lives that is 'not of God', we are not, in reality, actually serving Him because the true motivation for our actions is not God's glory: it is our own self-interest and vainglory. In effect, we make God our servant. It may be startling to think of it like this, but, nevertheless, this is exactly how we treat God at times.

Every battle against the forces of evil, for the salvation of souls, must be fought through an instrument of human reparation, that is, through a human being. The entire battle is about safeguarding this passing life for the sake of the eternal. The devil knows that by corrupting man in his material affairs he also weakens him spiritually, thus making it easier to lead him to perdition. Satan understands how short our material existence is and knows just how easily seduced we are by the world.

We might wonder why Satan is so obviously focused on perverting and corrupting the youth in particular. The reason for this is that he knows, that in their more tender years, souls are especially susceptible to his corrupting influence. It is, sadly, all too common nowadays to hear of young people committing suicide, or becoming addicted to drugs, sex, money and vice of all kinds. Young people are relentlessly bombarded by satanic influences through a whole variety of channels: the media; fashion; literature; music and art. When we are caught up in Satan's snares in our youth, it is much more difficult for us to free ourselves as adults and return to the path of goodness.

We see today the emergence of certain socio-cultural phenomena, which are both unprecedented and alarming. As never before, the youth wield huge influence in the areas of art, music, sports and technology. Many amass great fortunes at an early age resulting in great social and political power being conferred on irresponsible and immature individuals who, more often than not, are living lives mired in sin, enslaved to materialism and completely devoid of God. They want to construct a new church; the church of earthly powers. This is, in fact, the church which Satan offered Jesus when he tempted him in the desert (Luke 4:5-8).

In time, these callow youth, with their unbridled power, will grow increasingly contemptuous and hostile towards God and His people and their mocking, derisive attitude will only draw them deeper and deeper into the darkness.

Assimilating the Truth

We have reached a critical stage in history, and our situation is really quite urgent. We cannot just sit idly by waiting for God to manifest His Will in signs and wonders. The sign has already been given. As Jesus told us:

> "An evil and adulterous generation seeks for a sign, but no sign shall be given to it except the sign of Jonah". (Matt. 16:4)

We know what is good and what is evil. We know God's law and His commandments. We have our Faith and our doctrine, so we have no excuses. Our sincere conversion must brook no delay now because the battle is reaching fever pitch. It is no longer a matter of choice. It is time to forget ourselves and fight, with all our might, for God's Kingdom.

In these times, the forces of evil boldly present themselves in the full light of day. They no longer hide in the shadows. Those who stand courageously to proclaim and witness to the Kingdom of God will enjoy the protection of God's holy angels, whom He sends to protect His people. Those who are ashamed of the Gospel will not have this protection.

If we are to be active in the gifts of the Holy Spirit, it is necessary that we have a mystical conception of the responsibilities God the Father has assigned us, in His Son. Beginning with the Gospel, we must take care to make absolutely certain that we are living according to the truth it reveals. Any uncertainty or ambiguity on our part in regard to these truths makes us vulnerable. We become a direct target for enemy forces. When we are not fully active in the Christian Faith which we received at Baptism, we are letting down our guard, spiritually speaking. Then, the Evil One will attempt to destroy us. His attacks are much more concentrated, in fact, than those experienced by the unbaptized; those who do not belong to Christ. Ours is not a time for half measures. Baptism lays upon us certain responsibilities which we must acknowledge and face up to. Being Catholic is a vocation; it is a genuine call from God.

This call to follow Christ is an act of the Divine Will. It is not by any human will that we become Catholic. It is by God's grace. Being Catholic is not some accident of chance or quirk of fate. As Saint Paul tells us, we were chosen by God the Father for His Son, Jesus. Even those who come into the Catholic Church late in life were, in fact, chosen by the Father from all eternity. Only God, the Creator of everything, can call someone into His Church. What a great mystery and what a great honor this is! How and why a particular soul comes to belong to the Church is a unique and inscrutable mystery of God. It is something that is simply beyond the capacity of the human mind to comprehend.

It is important to discover what it actually means to be spiritual. The essence of being a true Catholic is recognizing oneself, first of all, as a spiritual being. It is only with the awareness that we are spirit, as well as flesh, that we can hope to confront an invisible, spiritual enemy that was created superior to us in many ways. Despite our seeming inferiority, it is also very important that we understand the power that we actually have within us. The fact is that, owing to the miracle of the Incarnation of Our Lord Jesus Christ, we are capable of bringing down great empires of evil.

Jesus became a man and freed us from the devil. He paid the debt due to original sin with His own Blood. So, it should be clear, then, that we require supernatural means to combat our enemy. We cannot win a single battle unless we receive the grace to do so. We live on this earthly plane as spiritual human beings, embodied souls. Whether baptized or not, everyone has a soul. This is a simple fact that will never change regardless of what anyone might think or believe. The truth is that the invisible is the permanent reality and the visible one, merely temporary.

We are spiritual beings in temporary exile, in a material state. The soul is initiated here in the lesson of love. Love is the power that makes it possible for us to transcend to the eternal promise of salvation, which is given to every Christian by the Lord Jesus.

We must submit to the laws of God, in obedience to his commandments, but this is something that seems to be becoming more and more difficult for human beings today. People now are so far from the truth that they are no longer able to comprehend the language of the spirit, or even conceive of obedience to an invisible God. It is sad to see so many Catholics nowadays who are so weak in the Faith that they are actually ashamed of their religion. Catholicism has become a threat to the secular world and something absolutely absurd in today's culture of death.

Preparation to Serve

To understand our Faith more deeply and find our place in it, it can be helpful to begin by considering how the Catholic Faith came to us in the first place. There are Catholics who were initiated through an inter-generational heritage, which may have existed for many centuries. These are often baptized soon after birth and are known as 'Cradle Catholics'. And then there are those who are called later in life, under very different circumstances. The moment of Baptism marks the true spiritual beginning of a person. The seeds of the Christian life reside in this holy sacrament. It exorcizes us from every bond to *Original Sin* and from every evil influence that comes down to us from our ancestors.

It is obvious when a Catholic has been called at a very young age to an active and committed life in the Church. He is distinguished in his discipline and holiness, and possesses a willingness to obey the law of God and a genuine fear of the Lord (Matt. 11:30). The life of such a Catholic has a resounding impact on the Church's spiritual battle with the empire of evil. Those called so early in life come to life ideally equipped to be those effective instruments of God, in Whose hands they become powerful weapons against evil.

We are all called to be fully active in the Church at different stages of life. For some, the call may come shortly before they depart this mortal coil. Others are unable to hear the call because they are asleep in the dream of this life. Those who are called later in life go through an enormous interior struggle. They have to constantly battle against the forces of evil because the enemy knows they are chosen by God for a specific purpose. They must confront an enemy who recognizes them as a potential threat and who may have an awareness of the individual's mission, although he himself may not yet be completely conscious of it. He must fight in a silent and mysterious battle against an enemy that seeks to drag him down into the deep waters of the material world, to destroy him before he becomes fully aware of God's plan for him. However, something deep within will continue to reassure him of the special mission he is called to fulfill in life.

We may wonder why God does not allow His chosen ones to have a clear knowledge of the mission for which He created them or of the nature of their late call to ministry. The truth is that God does, in fact, reveal to each of His children all the instructions they need for battle. Through the Deposit of the Faith, Sacred Scripture, Sacred Tradition and Church doctrine, He provides all the information, guidance and warnings we need to defend ourselves against the assaults of the enemy. By being vigilant, humble and obedient to the Holy Will of God, we become well-trained, highly effective soldiers of God's militia, and lethal weapons in the struggle against the enemy of souls.

The basic call of all the baptized is to be faithful to God and obedient to His laws. We must always be attentive to the Lord's voice and ready to answer His call, whether it asks us to enter more fully into the mission for which He created us, or to cross the threshold into eternal life. The Gospel establishes clearly the requirements of Christian duty and responsibility, but the

Christian today faces unparalleled, monumental challenges in his fight to resist the siren voices of materialism, consumerism, and relativism. Their seductive allure is, indeed, difficult to withstand, pandering as it does to his senses and instincts and swaying his intellect with compelling arguments to justify a life of comfort and ease.

Nowadays, many Catholics lack basic spiritual awareness. Their faith has become so watered-down that it can no longer be said to be truly Catholic. In point of fact, it more closely resembles that of the Christian sects; fraught with theological error and riven with religious confusion. This has left the elect more vulnerable than ever to the snares of the devil.

Perhaps more than ever before in history, there is an urgency now in the call to be vigilant. Our Christian duty demands that we stay awake and keep watch, shaking off the languor and inertia that grips us. Those who are active in the Church, as well as those who have been notably inactive up until now, are being called to prepare and to make themselves available for active service in the vineyard of the Lord. This very availability will make them watchful sentries and constitutes an intimidating presence which can halt the advance of enemy forces.

Even if we are not aware of our spiritual strength or our power against the enemy, we are still doing our part in the battle by virtue of the fact that we are the people of God. This alone places us in a commanding position; the enemy has no power over any territory we are defending. It is like a well-armed guard standing at the door of a jewelry store. Just by being there he is a deterrent to any would-be robbers. The store is no longer an easy target. The guard does not need to know which individuals passing by the store are thieves and which are not. His strong, watchful presence provides all the security the business needs.

It is exactly the same with the children of God. When we are watchful and standing guard at our post, we are defending the territory of souls entrusted to us. The guard post which God assigns us is the ordinary circumstances of our daily life; a life which is to be lived out in accordance with God's Holy Will, with no particular awareness of how things are working spiritually. Saint John, the beloved, gives us a beautiful example of this. On Jesus' way to Calvary, John was able to accompany him, right to the foot of the cross and to witness Jesus' crucifixion and death - despite the fact that he did not understand. All he knew was that his master was God. He had seen Jesus transfigure; he had seen his miracles first hand. How absurd it must have seemed to him, knowing that Jesus was God, to witness this God allowing Himself to be humiliated, tortured and put to death by His creatures. John was able to accept it all as something that was necessary, only because of his love for his Master and his faithfulness to God's Holy Will.

This is the way our own faith needs to be. This is how our heart must be disposed, its beats counting out the rhythm we must keep as we row through the waters of this earthly life. To cross over safely, we must arm ourselves with the sacraments of the Church and face up to the trials of life with courage, drawing consolation from knowing that we belong to the victorious army and to the One who is the *True Power*.

God's call means being open to the gifts of the Spirit. Being faithful to God activates these gifts and yields abundant fruit in the spiritual struggle of the *Militant Church* on earth. It is God's angels who are the guardians of these gifts. Although we cannot see the spiritual world, because of our material nature, it is a world that is protected by the spirits of God, who, as part of the family of God to which we also belong, are very much on our side. When facing hostile spiritual forces, they come to aid us, supplying that which we are lacking in order to be fully effective. Uniting with this spiritual reality leads a Christian on the path of goodness and develops within his heart the seeds of truth that were planted at Baptism. Being active and faithful to God, then, involves harmonious collaboration with the Heavenly Host; the saints and the holy angels of God.

In union with the spirits of God we form a perfect body; one in which there is no darkness. As intellectual bodies, the spirits act through our senses, instincts and imagination and may also communicate with us in the realm of our dreams. They work with all the intellectual information that we have assimilated in life. They have a wide sphere of operation within us, in which they are able to assist us even in the smallest details of our daily lives. They cannot, however, invade our privacy nor will they act in any area of our being unless we are trying to obey God's law and commandments, because they are in perfect harmony with the Holy Will of God. It is important to realize that *Original Sin* has diminished human nature and that, owing to its mortality, it is imperfect. Uniting with God's angels compensates for this lack, strengthening the people of God and transforming them into a true spiritual unity with God.

The Saints are also united to the army of God's angels. As soon as we enter into God's glory, we become part of this army and united to the holy angels. This is why, in his discussion with the Sadducees on the subject of resurrection, Jesus says: "They are like angels" (Matt. 22:30). Our guardian angel belongs to a choir of angels. He has a particular spirituality which corresponds to the spirituality which God has chosen for us. He is the light that will guide us through the desert of this earthly exile until we reach the fullness of God's Kingdom. The moment the soul enters the eternal dwelling of the Glory of God, it is united permanently to the angelic choirs. This does not mean, however, that we become angels - we have been created to be human beings for all eternity - but, it does mean that we will become perfect, just as they are.

A true understanding of the mystery of the Mystical Body of Christ is beyond human comprehension. We must simply abandon ourselves to that mystery and trust God, obeying Him despite our being unable to completely understand the mysteries of the Faith. This places us in an exalted position because it unites us to the Heavenly Father and leads us directly to the heavenly formation where the Holy Will of God will become ever clearer.

God's Invisible Power

The greatest joy for Heaven is to see a human being on earth who is faithful to God and who strives, using invisible weapons against an invisible enemy, despite being unable to see the spiritual world. This is a truly wonderful spectacle to behold because it is a vision of holiness, one which could never be achieved outside of God's Holy Will. It is a supernatural gift, a miracle of the redemption that comes to us in Jesus Christ.

To be in contact with the spiritual forces of Good requires an act of faith. Such an act enables us, as mere mortals, to become laborers in the vineyard of God's Kingdom. Being active in this spiritual militia means confronting the forces of evil and joining the battle, in union with God's angels, for the salvation of souls.

Even the smallest of God's children on earth is able to defend himself against the greatest giants of hell when he fights in perfect obedience to the Lord Jesus. Great, indeed, is the power given to God's army against Satan's forces. This should come as no surprise. We read in Sacred Scripture that, "David prevailed over Goliath with a stone" (1 Sam. 17:48-52). If we could only know just how powerful the army to which we belong really is, we would be filled with immense faith, courage and joy.

The world seduces us in such a way that it makes us lose much of the precious time we have on earth. This is all part of the enemy's strategy to deplete the strength of God's children and to make us lose sight of the great gifts of our Faith. Seeing God's grandeur being casually ignored by so many Christians, who are bedazzled by the attractions of the world, is tragic. It is like seeing Jesus being crucified all over again.

When we find our place within the destiny that God has mapped out for us, we discover the most important thing in life: our mission. Discovering God's plan for our lives means accepting that God knows everything, that He can do everything and that He is really the only One who is. Such an awareness helps us to abandon ourselves to His Holy Will which, in turn, brings us the peace and the security of knowing that He has the perfect plan for us and that we are under His loving protection.

What does it mean to abandon ourselves to God's Will? This abandonment means believing that Jesus is Lord and confessing our faith in him. It means accepting the mysteries of the Catholic Faith without reserve and obeying the precepts of the Church, even when we do not completely understand them. It is to follow the teachings of the Gospel as the absolute Truth by which we are to live. It is to subject ourselves to the Ten Commandments revealed to Moses by God on Mount Sinai. It is to understand doctrine as a map and a compass that gives direction to our life in the pilgrimage of our earthly exile. It is to accept that we must live pious lives untainted by the world and free from the slavery of the flesh's disordered passions. It is to belong completely to God and not to the devil and the world.

By being fully conscious and completely submerged in the knowledge of the Faith, we will be able to follow the steps of Our Savior, Jesus Christ, and to overcome all the obstacles we encounter on the way. To have found the Catholic Faith consciously is to have had a personal experience with Jesus Christ; a renewal in which the entire content of the treasury of the Faith begins to make perfect sense to the soul and to the heart. This draws us to live a life with God where everything centers on Him and aims at His glory.

Discovering the power of the Catholic Church is to find the true treasure. It is to recognize that God lives among us, walks with us each step of the way, enriching us with the wonderful gifts which He has bequeathed to us in the Holy Spirit.

The salvation of souls implies a real battle against the forces of evil. It is a battle that cannot be anticipated without perfect knowledge of the responsibilities that it entails. Here we enter a territory that calls for the most meticulous attention. We must prepare ourselves, in perfect obedience, to confront evil, taking care to ensure that we ourselves are not in sin. We cannot hope to exert any power over the devil when we are still in his territory. We can only confront the enemy by being completely faithful to God. Otherwise we readily fall prey to his seductions and are easily defeated by his wiles. We will always have to struggle against sin which nests in us. No matter how hard we struggle, we are bound to fall on occasion.

This is precisely why Jesus left us the sacrament of Confession, which he instituted when he breathed on the disciples saying, "Receive the Holy Spirit! Those whose sins you forgive, they are forgiven; those whose sins you retain, they are retained." (Jn. 20:22-23). It was so that we could be reconciled with him as soon as possible and regain our spiritual strength.

Through Christ's power, working through the Priest in this wonderful sacrament, we are able to restore our relationship with God and immediately recover our spiritual strength. Of course, it is also important that we always do our very best to resist sin by remaining vigilant and by being disciplined with ourselves.

To understand the language of spiritual warfare, it is necessary to truly comprehend what it means to engage in the battle. Without this awareness, spiritual warfare becomes an abstract intellectual notion, something we grasp only at a very superficial level. On this view, it is not experienced as a true reality. This, of course, is spiritually devastating for us, but, sadly, this is typical of the mentality we find in the Church today. Clergy are, very often, skeptical about the supernatural vision of the Gospel, even when they have been properly instructed in doctrine and law as necessary academic requirements of their priestly formation.

The Weapons of Faith

Before aligning ourselves fully with God's army, we need to be aware of the magnitude of the responsibility this places us under. We must be people of righteousness, firmly resolved to avoid evil; those who belong totally to God and who have no dealings of any sort with the darkness. To compromise even slightly on this means, effectively, that we are really serving ourselves and our own agenda. This weakens our defenses, enables our foe to snatch away our weapons and leaves us completely exposed to enemy attack.

What are the weapons of a Catholic?

The Catholic's primary weapons are the Precious Blood of Christ and the holy sacraments which are the pillars of the Church; the gifts of the Holy Spirit to the people of God. When He suffered and died on the Cross, Jesus paid the price of our redemption with His blood. Through God's love and mercy, we are pardoned and drawn to that extraordinary power that defeats all darkness: the Holy Eucharist. In the Eucharist Jesus has left us his Body and Blood to be our food, our strength, and the most effective of weapons for combatting evil and protecting the spiritual territories assigned to us. The sacraments supply us with fortitude, vigor and vitality to sustain us as we journey through this temporal life to our homeland in Heaven.

When and how do we join the spiritual battle?

When a Catholic receives his First Holy Communion, he fully engages in the Church's spiritual battle against evil, an evil which has besieged his soul from his Baptism. The influence of this evil is limited, to a large extent, by means of the grace and extraordinary protection God grants His adopted children in the sacrament of Baptism. When they receive their First Holy Communion, souls reach the age of reason and become responsible for their sins. Once they have been nourished by Jesus' Holy Body and Blood, communicants become instruments of Christ; vessels of reparation. The life and actions of a Catholic are established in the power of the Eucharist. When they enter the transcendental mystery of transubstantiation and receive Holy Communion, Catholics are joined mystically to the Lord's Passion, Death and Resurrection and become sharers in the intentions of Jesus' Sacred Heart. These intentions constantly guide the spiritual battle of the whole of humanity.

Because we live a life that is Eucharistic, one that is mystically nourished by the Body and Blood of Jesus, we are transformed by the Eucharist into living stones of God's Temple. If we could fathom the depths of this mystery or grasp its transcendental dimension we would be in ecstasy. A Catholic living a true Eucharistic life becomes more and more Christlike as the effects of the Body and Blood of Jesus transform his entire being. The more often one receives Holy Communion, the more deeply one is able to enter into the Lord's Passion and the more one is prepared for the real resurrection. The Eucharistic miracle transforms the person in the core of his being and gives him the strength to subjugate the passions of the flesh and to remain obedient to the Spirit.

As a Eucharistic instrument, a Catholic is called to follow Jesus with his eyes fixed, in hope, on the horizon of salvation. He is like the biblical Lot who obeyed God's instruction not to look back as he was led out of Sodom and Gomorrah, shortly before they were engulfed by the fire of God's wrath. (Gen. 19:15-22)

To be a faithful child of God implies that we fully understand the responsibilities placed on us by our Baptism. Once he comes into the fullness of the gift acquired through this sacrament, and as long as he remains obedient to God, he is invincible. Nothing can stand in the path of a disciple of Christ who takes up his spiritual weapons with confidence and conviction. If God's children could only know the power He gives them through Jesus, the whole of humanity would want to know Him and would immediately convert to Catholicism.

Very few of God's chosen children fully appreciate the gifts of the Spirit. Most have some basic understanding of the Church teaching but it remains largely an abstract concept, not a lived experience. This is why the message of the Gospel does not flow as freely today as it did in the days of the early Church. It also explains why we have so few martyrs today; those Christians who dutifully take up front-line positions without question, without fear and, like Lot, without a backward glance. Today's Church is lacking the spirit of martyrdom because she lacks Eucharistic strength. Because she does not commune as she ought with the Bread of Life, the Church is seriously undernourished. She is very rational and intellectual today, but does not have the strength or missionary zeal needed to sow the seeds of the Gospel with conviction.

As part of the Christian militia, one's life must be lived in the heart of the Gospel and in strict obedience to the precepts of the Church. This is a basic requirement for a Catholic as he journeys through life because one who does not obey the authority of the Church is unfaithful and will inevitably perish in the battle. The supernatural life of Christ's militia involves many sacrifices, but it is also enriched by the many consoling graces that God lavishes on us each day. It is a life which is no longer directed by mere external human events. Rather, it is directed by the love of God. It is a life lived in harmony with the spirit of the beloved disciple, Saint John, who walked with his Master every step on his dolorous way to Calvary, accompanying him right to the bitter end.

Taking up one's spiritual weapons, and having the awareness of the power they contain, already constitutes a victory over hostile forces who do not dare to confront such a formidable opponent. A faithful Catholic, regularly drawing from the treasury of the Eucharist, is a living tabernacle of the Holy Spirit. No demon, no power of evil can withstand the light he radiates.

God's army appears insignificant in the eyes of the world and passes unseen before the unbelieving. Sadly, today we find many Catholics who do not believe that Christ is truly alive in the Eucharist, because they do not have enough faith. To become a Eucharistic instrument a Catholic must have the faith necessary to consciously conceive of the mystical reality of the Presence of God in that tasteless bread, and of His Precious Blood under the appearance of wine; the natural made supernatural by the mystery of transubstantiation.

Initially, we believe in God through the gift of faith which God gives us, but this must be fanned into a flame. To the extent to which we succeed in developing this faith, we grow stronger spiritually and are able to live the supernatural anointing given to us by the Holy Spirit. We grow and develop in wisdom just as, "Jesus increased in wisdom and in stature, and in favor with God and man" (Luke. 2:52). Just as he made himself a perfect man even though he was God, (Heb. 2:7), so each one of us gains in wisdom and perfection to the extent that we walk in faithfulness to God, constantly battling to resist Satan along the way.

The forces of darkness will reveal themselves gradually to the extent to which we engage in the battle. The deeper we plunge into battle, the more disciplined and alert we need to be. The warrior's senses must be honed and constantly on the look-out for enemy traps. Once we are able to recognize how the devil operates, we are better equipped to defend ourselves from his attacks and to recognize his treacherous schemes. Just being aware of Satan, then, is the first step to becoming effective in the spiritual battle.

Unmasking the activity of Satan and his forces leads inevitably to conflict. He is like a snake hiding in long grass; difficult to spot and very easy to step on. One thing is for sure - if we do step on him, confrontation is sure to follow. He will attack without mercy and try to destroy us. His ultimate objective is to steal away our very soul from God. How can we defend ourselves against so powerful an enemy? How can we defeat the old serpent, Satan? Simply by being faithful to God and defending the works of goodness, we will have all the protection we need and the devil cannot touch us.

Where do we find this battle in our everyday lives?

Whenever we confront evil directly, by denouncing a crime, an infidelity or some corrupt practice, for example, we are unmasking the enemy. We soon find ourselves in a fierce battle, as all hell, literally, breaks loose. These territories of sin lie within Satan's domain; he guards them ferociously and in a spirit of vengeance, hatred and violence.

It is common to see such battles played out within the Church itself: when homosexual activities in seminaries are brought to light; or a pedophile is unmasked in a parish; or heretical preachers are reported; or when we see Church officials corrupted by money, or convents destroyed by nuns who practice New Age. All this involves us in a terrifying spiritual battle, because these areas belong to Satan and are under the complete control of his forces. It is inevitable, then, that we will face the full brunt of the enemy's assault. The luke-warmness of many Catholics nowadays makes them weak in the face of the many grave sins beleaguering the contemporary Church. Because they are so spiritually undernourished, they lack strength, conviction and courage and their fear of repercussions silences them, allowing evil to run amok. In this way, they lose the blessing of martyrdom.

Response to a Weakened Church

The Catholic Faith is a spiritual army that defends souls from Satan's power. The fact that She wages battle against the army of the underworld is no recent revelation. Saint Paul describes this reality vividly in his letter to the Ephesians (Eph. 6:12). Defending souls has always been the Church's primary role.

Many in the Church today, however, have lost the sense of the supernatural. Clergy have grown increasingly skeptical with regard to the spiritual world. They have become so rationalistic and institutionalized that the Church now seems more and more like just another corporate, secular establishment. Thankfully, we do still have many faithful clergy living under obedience to Church Doctrine and Sacred Tradition, but these are in the minority. They are part of the remnant of the people of God situated within the ranks of the clergy and religious. The 1960′s culture of materialism brought a devastating impact on vocations in the Church. Much seminary teaching has been corrupted by the pernicious influence of heterodox theology and outright heresy. This has resulted in, what we might call, the doctrinal malformation of many Priests, turning them into blind guides, to the great impoverishment of the lay faithful.

In India's seminaries, for instance, many of the Catholic clergy have been educated in an environment where Hindu culture and religion holds sway. Hindu elements, such as Hatha Yoga (or 'yoga exercises', as they are known in the West), and meditation techniques have been introduced into Divine Liturgy. Even in more traditional seminaries and schools, we are witnessing widespread liturgical abuses. Bishops are having their seminarians educated in secularized universities where they are formed without a community life, among people who are not with God and whose aims are entirely worldly. Obviously, a seminarian formed under these circumstances is unlikely to make a good priest. He becomes just another professional, with an entirely earthly focus, lacking a proper sense of God. Sadly, there are many such priests in our parishes today.

What a great grace it was for the Church to have been blessed for almost eight years with the pontificate of a Pope like Benedict XVI; a man who gave his entire life to serving the Church in unswerving obedience, with an extraordinary clarity of thought and with such a wonderfully rich and wholesome theology. He spoke to us with the pedagogy of God the Father, directing the Church on the path which She urgently needed to follow. It was most saddening during those years to witness the level of disobedience and indifference on the part of so many clergy and religious communities to the direction and guidance of this wise and courageous shepherd.

This fact alone points to a form of spiritual bankruptcy in a great part of the Church. It illustrates well how prevalent individualism, independence and pride are in the Church today. How can shepherds who are completely incapable of obeying, or of allowing themselves to be led, ever hope to become effective leaders of God's people? The Church of today stands weakened by those power structures, pseudo-hierarchies and

Catholic clergy who have 'liberated' themselves and who follow only human ideologies which are directly opposed to the call of the Gospel. They can no longer even conceive of what it means to be 'one body' made up of many members. The resulting fracturing of the Mystical Body of Christ, and rejection of unity, represents a protestantization of the Catholic Church.

Our unhappy depiction of the Church today may be of little concern to those caught up in the problems outlined here, but our observations do serve to highlight the extent of the damage the that Evil One has managed to inflict on the Mystical Body of the Church. This alarming state of affairs only matters, and indeed, only makes sense, to those who are living in the truth. They alone will have a genuine concern for the spiritual health of the Church. Only they will be able to recognize the full enormity of the battle now facing us. This is a reality to which we all need to quickly waken, because the enemy now stands within the very gates of the Church. We must be alert, coherent and courageous as we are to begin the work of exorcizing the great evil that now nests in the heart of the Church. Arming ourselves with prayer, holiness and compassion towards all members of the Church, we must go in search of those who have turned away from the truth and who are doing much harm to souls and, by so doing, also endanger their own salvation. We are called to be fishers of men, who catch the souls of our brethren, snatching them away from the devil. We act in the hope that, with God's grace, these brothers and sisters will repent and be saved.

The Eucharist is our greatest weapon. However, it is only when our whole being has been consecrated to the Blood of the Lamb, and when we strive wholeheartedly to be conformed to Christ and resolved to be done with sin forever, that we can receive the fullness of the Eucharist's gifts and power. Only then do we become instruments of God's grace; ready, willing and able to free our neighbors from the devil's chains and lead them back to the safety of the Church. Today, being faithful and being good are not enough. The Christian has to be courageous, and ready to lay down his life if necessary.

We are here to illumine the pilgrims who, while crossing the turbid waters of exile, go astray, losing the anchor of God and sink into the depths of materialism. They thereby break away from the moorings of their spiritual nature and become completely 'of the flesh' and 'of the world'. This is the most common experience of this earthly existence for multitudes who choose to separate themselves from God, the source of life.

What a huge responsibility has been placed in our hands, but are we even aware of it? We have been given the necessary knowledge and tools and the most effective weapons to defend and nourish souls. Our Christian duty demands the very highest levels of discipline. It is only by striving for perfection, which is holiness, that we can hope to fulfill the mission for which we were created (1 Thess. 4:3). None of these exacting demands will unnerve the true Catholic. They are no more than the obligations enjoined on us at Baptism. When we are faithful to our Baptismal vocation, we are automatically submerged in the realm of obedience that prepares us for the mission ahead.

The times in which we live demand that we be sober and vigilant. There is no place today for idle speculation or argument, or for dabbling in the cults and practices of our neighbor, practices which do not belong to the true religion revealed to us directly by God Himself. We have the truth. We must have nothing to do with spiritual fairy tales, pagan belief systems or occult or exotic-sounding New Age ideas. We cannot allow ourselves to be swayed from the truth by pseudo, 'feel-good christianities' which are devoid of sacramental foundations and which seek to seduce us at the emotional level with stirring speeches. Only our inheritance, an inheritance that comes to us directly from Jesus Christ, the Lord, contains the fullness of revealed truth. In His great love and compassion, Christ has given His Church all the gifts necessary for salvation. He has ensured that She lacks nothing. It is our duty to remain faithful to the Truth and to the heritage which we have been blessed to receive.

The social networks serve up on a silver platter some of the most common temptations for the rational and unspiritual clergy and laity of today. They present a syncretism that is so subtle and seemingly innocuous that it is all too easy to be deceived. It seems totally harmless on the surface but it is not long before its insidious effects start to manifest. It can bring about a gradual deterioration in the integrity of one's faith that may result in serious, even harmful consequences. New Age practices are a common example. We often see their rapid proliferation in parishes, seminaries and religious communities, and the great spiritual damage to individuals and communities that follows in their wake.

There are many problem areas in the Church today; areas of darkness that urgently need to be tackled. They must be brought out into the light and unequivocally denounced. We must move with solidarity, in one spirit, living the same truth and bearing the same weapons. Otherwise, we will lack the necessary discernment to distinguish spirits, a gift which is so vitally important for today's spiritual warfare.

We are responsible for our actions and for safeguarding our own spiritual lives as well. To this end, we must be careful who we associate with and with whom we choose to keep company. The light can have no truce with the darkness, nor children of the light with children of the darkness. In general, we should not maintain friendships with persons who are not in obedience to God. There are, of course, exceptions to this, for example, when we are evangelizing, or seeking to rescue souls from the devil to bring them back to God, as is often the case with family members, work colleagues and members of our parishes.

Some preachers today look for modern ideas that will make them appear 'with it'. Their curiosity can quickly hurtle them down dangerous roads as they covet after fame, power and human approval. It is vital that we, as imitators of Christ, hold fast to the true Faith, to our heritage and Sacred Tradition; that we emulate the acts of the apostles after Pentecost, when they were filled with the Holy Spirit. For, if we do not, we will not survive spiritually. We will not be able to obey God's commands because our ears will become deaf to His instructions.

A prominent feature of how the battle is being fought today is the substitution of the truth for what is popular. The effects of this are devastating in the Church. The enemy of the soul mines our lines with modernist, people-pleasing ideologies which lead to confusion, rancor and debate. Immutable truths of the Faith and Church teaching are challenged and proposed as topics for discussion. This alone is a very grave error. The day that a virgin sits to discuss her virginity, might well be the end of her virginity or the beginning of its end. The day we discuss our honesty might well be the day we become dishonest. The truth should not be debated or discussed. It is to be proclaimed, announced, exalted, cherished, and preached as a reality, as fact. Otherwise, what would be the meaning of the Cross? What would be the sense in the Lord's crucifixion and death?

If it is acceptable to discuss the truth and to debate it in an arena that seeks to disprove it, then martyrdom has no meaning or purpose. Christ's death would have been completely unnecessary. He could have discussed it with Pontius Pilate, and Herod, and come to a mutual agreement. He could have initiated a dialogue with those Jews who did not believe him and explained to them how He was, in fact, really their friend. At the end of his dialogue with Jesus, Pontius Pilate, famously asks; "What is truth?" (John. 18:38). Jesus does not enter into a discussion with him on truth. He remains silent. The truth speaks for itself.

The meaning of Christianity is transcendental. It is a truth that invites us to walk in one direction: Golgotha. There can be no deliberating in the face of doctrinal truth; there can be no debate about dogma. Dogma is not open to discussion; it is simply to be believed and unconditionally accepted, as true. By means of Her precious and inerrant teachings, Mother Church gathers her brood under her wings and leads them safely on the way of salvation.

The Spiritual Battle

Living the Faith in a spiritual way means accepting the responsibility that has been given to us. We also need to have a mystical perception of the spiritual battle in which we are engaged, and to understand the nature of the enemy we face. It is common for people to live the Faith at the purely intellectual level, focusing only on material reality. To encounter those who live the Faith in a truly spiritual way is much more rare. But this is exactly what Jesus asks us to do. If our Faith is just about providing earthly comfort and refuge in times of difficulties, then the Gospel cannot be said to be truly alive in us.

Jesus clearly presents all aspects of this earthly life as a temporal state of being. Although we are in exile here in this lower world because of *Original Sin*, Christ promises to permanently liberate the faithful and lead them to paradise. By the grace of Jesus' Holy Incarnation, man's life, which was dead in sin, is transformed into an eternal life in the fullness of God's glory (Eph. 2:4-7). This is a revealed truth that we accept or reject. If we do disregard it, by choosing to live unspiritual lives, relying on religion alone to save us, our emaciated souls will be in great danger at the moment of death, when they enter into the fullness of the spiritual world.

To live a religious life that is not truly spiritual is to don the mantle of the Pharisees. Those who live such inauthentic lives claim to be 'of God' and to do everything in His name, but the reality is that they are only seeking their own interests and vainglory. This hypocrisy is, sadly, all too common in the Church today among religious, the clergy, and the laity. The lack of authentic spirituality is one of the main reasons for the lack of vocations in many parts of the Catholic world. Vocations will only flourish in the midst of communities where the Spirit of God is alive; among communities that believe in the family, who lead sacramental lives and who pray, fast and do penance. Vocations will never arise from human projects, ideologies and modernist theologies. They take root and grow by the gifts of the Holy Spirit, through Sacred Tradition and fidelity to Magisterial Teaching.

To be an instrument of Christ, it is necessary that we appropriate the full depth and richness of our Christian heritage and that we know the ways of the Gospel. A Christian who does not fully understand the nature of the spiritual battle is a soldier who already lies dead on the battlefield. As for those who refuse to obey the hierarchy of the Church, they will be trampled mercilessly underfoot by the Evil One and, perhaps, even destroyed. Since evil is hierarchical by nature, it will only recognize the hierarchical authority of the forces opposing it. To be outside of the hierarchical order is to be a soldier outside of his own ranks, extremely vulnerable to enemy attack. When Jesus gave Peter the keys of heaven, he conferred upon him the power to bind or loose, in heaven and on earth (Matt. 18:18). In so doing, he established a hierarchy in the early Church, headed by Peter and the apostles, who were given the authority to wield power against the forces of darkness. These forces, with the devil at their head, also form a hierarchy, comprised of angels from the different choirs who were thrown down to earth (Rev. 12:9). These form a hierarchy of disobedience which is ranged against the Army of God. They will only recognize the hierarchy of the Church, because She alone has been given the authority of Christ. Only the Catholic Church, the Church founded by Christ, has real power against the Enemy. No one else does.

The history of Christianity begins with the patriarchs and prophets of long ago. For many centuries, and in the midst of immense trials and battles, they announced the coming of the Messiah and prepared the way for Him. God's Incarnation was finally realized in the Annunciation of the Archangel Gabriel to Our Lady, the Virgin Mary. In the two thousand years since then, the people of God have continued this battle, as they journey through their earthly exile towards the Heavenly Jerusalem.

If we are going to fight in the open fields of the spiritual world as true Christians, we must stand within the ranks of Church hierarchy. When we do not fully accept Church teaching in its entirety, we are uprooted from our security. We become worthless chaff, 'worldlings' and playthings of the Devil. When we belong to God, He is our Lord. He alone is. We only are to the extent that He is in us. Without Him, we are nothing. Only with this degree of communion with God can we effectively combat evil.

It is very common today to find lay people leading deliverance ministries. Not all of them are in obedience to the Church or under the guidance of a priest. As we should very well know, deliverance ministries and exorcism are matters that must be handled with great care and prudence and always under the authority of the Church. This is because we are fighting against Satan and the demonic. If we are not lined up with the hierarchy, we get into deep trouble. This is why so many lay ministries are in danger. When priests are not reporting these ministries to their bishops, the devil gets involved, money and fame enter in and they lose their way, causing many problems within the Church.

Some lay people and priests do this job really well, working in obedience to the hierarchy of the Church. It is a magnificent and necessary ministry because we have so many people getting involved with New Age and all kinds of treaties of the dark. Often there is no help available because we have very few exorcists. There is a great need today for true deliverance ministry to be carried out, as it should be, under the authority of the Church.

When those carrying out a deliverance ministry do not have authority against the devil, the evil spirits that inhabit the possessed soul remain and they may choose to transform themselves into demonic germs. By invading the host's vital organs, they deprive them of the strength they need to pray and, in this way, the evil spirits effectively neutralize the effects of the prayers which have been tormenting them. Demons are unable to withdraw without the permission of the demonic prince whom they are obliged to obey. The demonic prince only answers directly to the Church in her hierarchical authority. Consequently, he will not manifest himself to an exorcist who is not in total obedience. If the demonic prince cannot be summoned, there can be no deliverance, because the spirits that have been enslaved in that soul, by his order, cannot withdraw until either the demonic prince orders them to, or the Church, through Her exorcist, compels him to withdraw with all his legions.

The devil will mock the disobedient and deceive them with a false deliverance. Tragically, the victims will suffer serious physical infirmities. Because they come directly from the spirit, the infirmities will constantly move from one organ to another throughout the body, making an accurate diagnosis impossible.

In these times, the devil's forces will manifest themselves in truly spectacular fashion. Christian magicians fill arenas around the world with religious sideshows and millions are deceived by the prodigies that the devil does through them. Major cures continue to impress the unwary and the curious. The whole sad phenomenon derives from a thirst for money, ambition for human power, pride and spiritual arrogance. These magicians reign supreme in Christian sects, and in some Catholic ministries, and will drag with them thousands upon thousands of luke-warm and inquisitive souls. We have an example of this in Peter's encounter with Simon the Magician. (Acts. 8:18-24).

The Devil's manifestations usually take root in individuals who are in search of attention, using the things of God. These will be the most attractive individuals of today's popular culture. We live in a world of artists, famous actors and celebrities, many of whom do not use their art for the good. We are not aware just how much we have been conditioned by modern technology. Audio-visual systems being used to promote commercial agendas, as well as electronic games and musical videos, engage our senses at such speed that we have had to re-adjust our sensory reception to cater for them. This has resulted in a sort of human reprogramming which has led inexorably to shorter attention spans. Cinema and television are created using a dynamic high-speed system which has made us impatient and intolerant, developing in us anxieties and serious states of neurosis. The communications media now represents one of humanity's main areas of focus, a principle source of education and a primary means of connection between people worldwide. In the best of cases, the media can be a powerful tool at the service of humanity's good; in the worst, it can be a deadly weapon aimed at humanity's destruction.

Our relationship with all modern communications media needs to be managed carefully. For many, they are a very useful tool, necessary for operating effectively in today's world. If not properly controlled, however, they can result in serious negative effects, causing great damage to the fundamental structure of the human person: the individual's interior health; his mental and emotional health; and, in many cases, even his physical health. We are now so conditioned by a short attention span, that we have become more intolerant, impatient and lacking in compassion. We are becoming a more hostile people - slaves of modern human sciences and therapies which have been cleverly designed to make us dependent - and all purely for financial gain. As a consequence of all of this, we are becoming weaker and weaker in the living out of our daily lives. The simplest and most basic daily demands have become more and more challenging and our lives a series of therapies and psychological experiments.

Most of the modern psychology 'industry' with all its psycho-therapies and techniques for overcoming *the self,* have been designed to make us dependent on those who appear to be guardians of health, but, in reality, are service providers. Our health has become just another commercial industry. By considering this perspective realistically and carefully, we can refocus. Standing on this ground, we will know what to do when the enemy confronts us. Only when we know the nature of the harm that such evil causes to its victims, are we able to use the weapons required for protecting souls: only then will we be able to prescribe the medicine needed.

The most effective way to rescue souls from a radical loss of grace, in today's culture of death, is to be conscious of the subtle tricks the devil uses to enslave them. His tactics are so old that most people do not detect them. They seem natural and ordinary because we have inherited them. They are part of the world into which we are born. With the first rays of the sun on the first day, they appeared and, when the sun hid itself, they remained. They seem to have always been there, a naturally occurring aspect of reality, but the truth is that they have been laid out as bait, by infernal predators, seeking to entrap unwary souls.

To the extent to which we are on guard and able to read the tell-tale signs left by the demons, the spiritual war will go our way. When we can recognize these signs, we are able to move around the battlefield unhurried. But, we must not allow ourselves to be deceived and our view of human nature must be clearly established in our minds. Our discernment must focus on a field where the enemy has been detected.

It is not natural to live in a world that is populated by forces that are doing their utmost to prevent our attaining salvation. It confounds us why our enemy is so intent on doing us harm and on obstructing our path to the heavenly kingdom. What is it that is lacking in these angels who, even though they were given the same freedom as us, and are superior to us, they still rejected God? The answer is love. The heart of the human, or angelic creature, who chooses to live outside obedience to

God, is completely devoid of love. Love and compassion only come from God.

Our enemy is the enemy of God, Satan, who was cast out of heaven and thrown down to earth; this same earth where we must spend our earthly exile. As Sacred Scripture tells us:

> "For the accuser of our brethren has been thrown down, who accuses them day and night before our God." (Rev. 12:10).

There is no forgiveness for Satan and the fallen angels. They know they will never be able to return to heaven, yet, despite our being inferior to them, going to heaven remains a possibility for us, if we obey God. This fills them with envy and rage and their hatred towards us will never end. It will blaze in the fiery abyss for all eternity.

The Seduction of the Devil

Humanity cannot live without God. Regardless of how many times it has tried to in the past, no empire, no cycle of humanity has survived when it has forsaken the laws of God.

Today we are part of a society which is evil, perverted and decadent. It seems to have reached rock bottom, spiritually speaking. It is hard to imagine that a greater darkness is possible. We are in a moment of history where each one of us is being called to effect a radical change in every aspect of our lives. We must adopt the highest values and moral principles if we are to recover the vast territories that have been lost to the decadence and immorality which have proved so devastating to humanity throughout history. Again and again, each generation, in its pride and blindness, falls into the same traps, unwilling or unable to learn from the mistakes of the generations that preceded them.

Looking around today, we see smoking fields put to the torch by the "flaming arrows of the Evil One" (Eph. 6:16). Skies are darkened by the great spiritual battle raging all around; we cannot escape its fury or hide from its ravages. The more fiercely the battle rages, the more ignored it seems to be by those who worship the things of the earth. The scene today is reminiscent of Jesus' description of how the world was just before the Great Flood (Luke. 17:27).

The Devil has always been expert at seducing people with the things of the world. So pleasing and intoxicating are the earthly delights he presents, that we are unable to detect the subtle scent of sulfur that might alert us to his satanic presence. He deceives our senses, making us deaf and blind. Consequently, we can no longer see the signs of the times. He diverts our attention from the eternal to the temporal plane, tuning our focus to purely transitory matters. He is like the thief who knocks on the car window of a passenger's door to distract him while his accomplice relieves the victim of his valuables through the opposite window.

It is a precept of the New Age law that creation and creatures are to be worshipped rather than the Creator. The spirit of Satan is creating a type of globalized religion today, aimed solely at the worship of ecology and the putative well-being of the planet. We have become so caught up in worrying about the destruction of the planet that we have stopped thinking about the destruction of souls. It is the ozone layer of the human heart that we should be concerning ourselves with. It has become so depleted by the sin in the world that the searing shafts of hell's fire are able to penetrate its protective layer, mortally wounding souls and destroying in them love, mercy and compassion. We are called to be more concerned with carbon emissions, climate change and cruelty to animals, etc. - which may be worthy enough issues in themselves - but all this is pointless when people's hearts continue to grow harder and harder.

We can see in the so-called 'developed' nations how important external appearances are. Aesthetics and physical beauty are everywhere to be seen; things are superficially so attractive and well-manicured. Everything is so tightly controlled that the law and order of which they are so proud is actually more like a police state. If we could see into the hearts of these governments and societies, we would see that they have, in fact, lost what is most precious: their values, their morals, their principles and their fear of God. People have exchanged revealed truth for Satan's lies. Perverse ideologies like homosexuality and feminism abound and evil laws such as abortion, euthanasia and same-sex marriage, aimed at the destruction of mankind, have become the order of the day. Pornography and promiscuity are promoted everywhere and laws against 'hate speech' limit the preaching of the Gospel. We already see in many 'developed' countries the public exhibition and worship of all sorts of depravity. Decadence reigns supreme in the heart of millions of dysfunctional families. The children whom they decide not to abort have been conceived in fornication. The moral climate has never been more poisonous and never before have souls stood in such direct and immediate danger of damnation. We have a very clear picture of a human family that has left the path. The human family has become a dysfunctional one and sin has become its 'normal' way of life.

As the human family enters this reign of disobedience, the natural order is disturbed and we risk calamity. Turned away from God, and in a state of disobedience, we lose God's protection and are deprived of the capacity to discern. Dark forces and terrible powers may suddenly arise with diabolical designs beyond our worst imagining, seeking the complete destruction of every human being; body and soul.

Before the beginning of World War II, man was still able to recognize the enemy and devise a strategy to combat the evil he saw in the world. That was, however, the last opportunity he had. I have had a very clear vision where I was able to comprehend that we are in the midst of what we might call a 'Third World War'; a war where we are unable to identify from whence the enemy is coming. Just when we think we have vanquished one evil, another, even worse, arises elsewhere in the world. This spiral of evil will continue to intensify and, as it does so, people's fear and alienation from God will deepen. Even as humanity's crises worsen, man will continue to grow more and more arrogant. He will show not the least sign of repentance nor will he be able to discern the source of his misfortunes. Governments will grant more and more powers to police forces as they seek to control people, thus depriving them of their privacy and their identity. Ultimately, this will bring about a total loss of human dignity.

All the advanced weaponry that man, in his pride, has developed since World War II will be proved by God to be completely redundant compared to the enormous power we have given the Evil One. God will put humanity on its knees using such simple and primitive means that the world's superpowers will be humiliated in the most absurd fashion. Finally, they will come to realize that God is speaking. By then, it will probably be too late. The world will be in shock. Man will be cowed but will lack the discernment or spiritual understanding to know what to do. The earth will be populated mostly by spiritually undernourished souls who are unable to love or forgive. Such souls have no compassion for others; their only interest is to exist in their own self-love. They are like islands trying to exist independently. They are lost creatures, attached solely to the material and without an eternal future in the kingdom of light. These are human beings who have been given all God's gifts, but have rejected them in favor of temporal goods.

It is no accident that the world's most widely-feted celebrities today are atheists and pagans. This illustrates well the extent of the idolatry the world has adopted. Openly rejecting God, and unencumbered by any restraint, such high-profile figures bear powerful witness to the satanic anti-Gospel. They embrace a moral relativism which is contemptuous of the very notion of objective truth. With Pilate, they might ask "What is truth?" (John. 18:38). Such a disposition places the human person in a state of total separation from God. Spiritually speaking, he is in a 'gypsy' state, navigating aimlessly through the spiritual world without the compass of the truth to guide him. In reality, he is deceived and lost in life but finds himself being satisfied with pagan notions and human ideologies. He is a slave to his passions and is unpredictable, never able to attain true peace or happiness. He feels a deep, empty void within, which he tries to fill with earthly pleasures and material success. But these will always come with a very expensive price tag. The powers of darkness will always exact their price, to the last penny. The consequences of such an ongoing association with 'The Prince of this World' as Jesus called him, can lead to damnation in an abyss of eternal darkness.

It is not just a question of realizing that people can be damned by their own choice. Is it that people do not know that hell exists or that they just do not want to know? Perhaps, some know and just do not care. Pagans, and others who do not know God, have not received the knowledge or the responsibility that Christians have. They do not know the truth. Christians, however, should know. They have no excuse. To know such truths and to be conscious of the reality of hell is not only a responsibility but a wonderful grace. If one really understands the dimension of this gift of believing in faith, one enters a state of heightened spiritual consciousness and this level will give an inner peace which is impossible to describe in human words, one which can only be conceived in one's spirit. When we are conscious of what God has given us, in the person of His Son, Jesus Christ Our Lord, then we are already free.

God has given us free will. He will never interfere with our freedom to choose a specific course, but this does not mean that we can stand idly watching the staggering multitude of souls who are heading directly for hell. In love, we must sound the trumpet of the Gospel, loud and clear, inviting everyone to the salvation won for us by Jesus, Our Lord. That is our duty, our mission as members of Christ's army.

The description offered here of the state of the crisis facing humanity today is not a fanciful notion. Our situation is, in fact, very grave indeed. God, in His mercy, is calling souls who wish to deepen their awareness of their earthly existence. He is calling them, above all, to obey the Church, to wake up and to recognize the seriousness of our situation. Our Lord is calling each of us to do what we must do in order to give direction to our communities and countries.

When we are so deeply immersed in the material world, our soul is so weak that it is unable to recognize spiritual language. A reflection of this sort on the true responsibilities of our life before God will be vexing, perhaps even offensive. But, for those who are living in the knowledge of these truths, it is important to speak about them unceasingly. Otherwise, how can we hope to help those who are entranced by the dazzling illusions of this passing life? We must exhort our brothers and sisters to the truth, in season and out of season.

We must work every day of our short earthly life to be genuine witnesses of hope in the eternal glory that is about to come. This is the promise to those who are willing to give their lives out of love for God. Although this God is invisible and intangible to our very fragile human existence in many ways, our love is very concrete and fills us with true joy and peace. God's infinite generosity to us, His children, is absolutely extraordinary. He refuses us no good gift, showering us with an abundance of grace, so that we can really become instruments of His glory, for which reason, He made us. This is what Jesus means when he says that if we believe that he is the Lord and follow his way, we will be able to do everything that he did, and even more. This is His promise and God does not lie.

Awakening the Church

We can think of the Catholic Church as a giant slowly beginning to stir. Unfortunately, the magnificent gifts the Lord has bestowed on her children will remain unopened by the vast majority. It is tragic that the preciousness of these squandered gifts will only become apparent to many after they have passed beyond the doors of death. They will lament to see all that they might have done to free many multitudes of souls from the chains of the devil but did not, simply because they lacked a proper appreciation of the spiritual world and the nature of the forces working against our salvation.

If we are incapable of grasping the fullness of what has been given to us, it is because of our tendency to fritter away our time on earth, chasing the wind, and living a fleeting, temporal illusion that leads nowhere and leaves us with nothing in the end. This tragedy is something absolutely bewildering for the soul, which will bitterly regret failing to complete the mission which it was put on earth precisely to carry out. They will be pained to see the opportunities they had to leave behind them what might have been a great spiritual legacy, namely, the means by which souls might have defended themselves.

These spiritual *means* are the tools and techniques that individuals develop, with the inspiration of the Holy Spirit, to help them survive their daily, spiritual battles. We are created by God as unique beings, with the capacity to produce highly effective, powerful spiritual tools for the benefit of ourselves and future generations. By means of this creative capacity, we are able to protect ourselves from the *Enemy of the Soul* and better exploit this present life for the benefit of our eternal salvation.

Every generation engages in a unique spiritual battle and develops a particular set of tactics for its particular struggle. The strategic knowledge accumulated by successive generations from these battles is considerable. It constitutes a veritable arsenal of weapons and tactics from which future generations, faced with comparable challenges, are able to draw.

Each and every exorcism, each cycle of struggle, battle, effort and trial of the people of God against Satan contributes to this important bank of information. It is a form of spiritual capital that sensitizes us to vast areas of demonic manifestations. The more we truly understand spiritual warfare, the quicker we will be to fend off the attacks coming against us, and the better able we will be to defend those the Lord has entrusted to our protection.

Every day when we wake up, the enemy's army has already taken up its position. We must locate and confront it in the certain knowledge that we will be strengthened for the battle by God. Our capacity to detect the position of our spiritual enemy will depend on how alert we are, and this, in turn, will depend on how faithful we are to God. Throughout our lives we must strive to remain spiritually awake. In Gethsemane, Jesus asks John, Peter and James, "Why do you sleep?" He exhorts them to, "Rise and pray that you may not enter into temptation" (Luke. 22:46). This tells us something of the discipline we need to cultivate in our lives. Jesus indicates plainly that we must not fall asleep. This is a lesson for each one of us and for those generations yet to come. Furthermore, it is one which we absolutely have to master, if we are to survive all the battles that still have to be fought before the Lord Jesus returns.

This conflict between Good and Evil will only end when Jesus returns and puts an end, once and for all, to the reign of death. For centuries, the Church has accumulated a vast wealth of knowledge and experience in exorcism and demonology, resulting from her myriad clashes with Evil. These powers of the dark, in their never-ending conflict with the militant Church, constantly need to revise their strategies and reinvent new, evermore dastardly schemes in their attempts to defeat the Church. Each cycle of humanity must learn to counteract these diabolical machinations. In so doing, they accumulate valuable new insights which can then be passed on to successive generations to augment the general deposit of the Church's specialized knowledge in the whole area of spiritual warfare. This knowledge provides useful insights, indications and guidelines to assist each new generation with its own particular battle, but, as with our foe, we too must continually strive to develop fresh tactics if we are to counteract the enemy's battle plans.

These strategies are graces that Jesus himself gives the Church, through the Holy Spirit. They are received by the individual cells of His Mystical Body, the living stones of the Temple of God, that is, by each one of us. As God's living witnesses, we must construct a solid spiritual edifice on the foundations laid by Our Lord. Because we are the living stones which have been laid on the foundation of Christ, we have an immense responsibility within the human family. This is a great spiritual gift but it also represents a special mission in its own right. The maintenance and transmission of these *spiritual strategies* down through the generations require a genuine love. The devil knows how to stir up jealousy and pride in the hearts of the faithful, so that the actions and victories of the past are downplayed or overlooked. Similarly, new innovative strategies are often rejected because they do not accord with traditional approaches or understanding. This creates a generation gap which results in a rejection of the spirit of renewal by the youth in the Church, who themselves are the bearers of important stratagems, given them by God, for the sake of continuing the spiritual battle in modern times.

These lost graces weaken the faithful, making them easy prey for the Church's enemies, such as the New Age cults and pagan philosophies that invaded the western Christian world in the 1960s. This provides a clear example of Satan's most recent strategy. For several centuries, the Church contested Islam. Then, it was Communism. Today her main enemies are syncretism and moral relativism, which are every bit as destructive as any foe the Church has had to face in the past. This is a stark reality to which the Catholic Church really needs to wake up. There is a spiritual battle raging all around us and it is one in which we are all engaged, whether we like it or not. We face major assaults on all fronts and only those who are strong in the Faith can hope to survive.

We see many traditional religious congregations today living in opulence, even decadence. We see hundreds of monasteries and parishes in desolation, their graces depleted. These do not produce vocations because they are mired in New Age practices which are directly inspired by Satan: the enneagram, yoga, reiki, spiritualism, meditation techniques and so many other things that only contribute to the destruction of the Faith and to the loss of thousands of souls.

We must return to a seminary formation which is in accord with the principles of Sacred Tradition, rather than those flowing from a modernist intellectualism, undergirded by fallacious ideologies centered in moral relativism, secularism and all sorts of outlandish philosophies which contradict the True Faith. Such deceptions lead straight to the abyss and have ensnared thousands of priests and nuns, particularly in the last century. These nefarious influences have resulted in thousands of Catholic clergy becoming mired in all kinds of dubious practices which directly violate Catholic Faith and practice.

There is hope, however. We see in the example of Saint Paul's conversion how Jesus makes all things new. When the Lord appeared to Saul, he infused in him, instantly, all the wisdom that he had imparted to his apostles over a period of three years. Just meditating on this episode alone can provide endless, wondrous insights into the mystery of Christ, Our Lord, who, in the Holy Eucharist, gives us the greatest of all spiritual gifts. This sacrament is the most powerful weapon against Satan, and is the most effective spiritual power given to us by the Lord. Jesus gave us the precious gift of His own Holy Body and Blood to be our food and drink so that we would never suffer spiritual hunger or thirst while crossing the desert of our earthly exile. The Lord also gives the gifts of the Spirit to his Church, but these need to be actualized, that is to say, manifested plainly in our daily lives, and in all aspects of our dealings with our neighbor, with ourselves and with God. These gifts are a call to love; to be love itself. To be love means to be forgiveness, and to be forgiveness means to live in God, which means to do His will. Once we grasp this, our responsibilities will increase and we will begin to acquire greater knowledge of the daily changes going on all around us, and in the whole of the human family. We will gradually come to discern that earthly life is in constant flux precisely because of the spiritual battle in which we are embroiled.

Although this battle is in some ways a subtle one, it is also the most devastating because of the vast numbers of souls that are being dragged to the abyss. Today a cacophony of different voices vie to be heard and the vast majority of them do not come from God. Confusion reigns. This is why it is more important than ever for us to be united as a Church. Only in this way can we hope to stand against the spirit of division, which is one of our greatest enemies. This spirit infiltrates the Church easily because of pride. This pride is the root of original sin and something that we might say is intrinsic in human nature. Even though we have been exorcized from the power of the devil through Baptism, the tendency to sin, that is in us, remains. This tendency is quiescent as long as we stay faithful to God but, when, in our weakness, we are assailed by the fire of temptations, it very quickly flares up to torment us.

In a pastoral context, these prideful tendencies can become all too obvious. The hierarchy may be unwilling to accept the spiritual gifts of the laity, and the laity, in their turn, may flatly refuse to obey legitimate Church authority. Such attitudes need to be examined carefully if we are to prevent the enemy from exploiting our weaknesses by sowing a spirit of pride and division in our ranks and this is no mean task, given the considerable number of Catholics who, in their confused state, oppose Church teaching and behave more like enemies of the Church than her faithful children.

If her spiritual campaign against the *Forces of Darkness* is to be effective, it is vital that the Church be humble and perfectly aligned in hierarchical obedience. She must also be open to embracing the new charisms that the Holy Spirit gives her through the *Ecclesial Movements* and *New Communities* who are often the bearers of the new weapons which God gives to combat the devil. We always keep in mind, of course, that Our Lord will always be our surest weapon. It is from him that all the power to combat and destroy evil emanates.

There is no time to lose. Too many people in the world are already on the road to hell. Today's battle demands that we turn away from mediocrity and embrace complete fidelity to God. We need to look at the heroic witness of Saint Paul and to seek to emulate him, and of Saint Peter, who asked to be crucified upside down. We have been given an immense number of souls to defend. We must take action. We must raise high God's banner and set out boldly on our march to conquer the prevailing evil of our times. We must fearlessly proclaim the truth, in all its fullness, and set the world on fire with the love of God.

Resisting the Forces of Evil

We must be at peace with God, trusting fully in His mercy, love, forgiveness and compassion. We also need to be responsible stewards of all the Lord has entrusted to us. This involves, in the first place, staying awake and alert and keeping watch for the enemy. We have to nourish our faith if we are to remain strong in spirit and able to bear the weight of the flesh and to resist the illusions of the world and the temptations of the devil. These will bring us down, steal our peace and rob us of our humility, rendering us much less effective as spiritual warriors. The gift of humility is crucial when confronting hostile forces because pride is Satan's dominion. Simply put, when we are ruled by *pride* we are ruled by Satan.

There are many voices clamoring to be heard today and most of them only leave us confused. We live in a world where the spirits of syncretism, relativism and materialism hold sway. These are gathered together in one body and that body is the anti-Christ. It may not seem immediately obvious, but these spirits are not independent or unrelated. They are, in fact, joined together, and work together with a singleness of purpose. The astrologer and tarot reader may operate in different continents, the reiki teacher and yoga instructor can be competing with one another in the same neighborhood, as can the spiritualist and the shaman. All these dark practices are, in reality, part of the same spiritual force opposing the Spirit of God. They are the forces of the anti-Christ.

Sexual impurity in the Church is one of the devil's favorite weapons, and priests and religious among his favorite targets. Once he brings them down, he is able to turn them into the vilest and most devastating instruments of evil to bring against the Church herself. A priest who is contaminated by impurity and has abandoned celibacy becomes a serious threat to the Church, because such a priest will often misuse his power to persecute those who are faithful and to lead God's sheep astray. Alas, sexually depraved priests and religious have already taken root in the Catholic Church. They start movements which they want accepted by the Vatican, and they demand to be accepted themselves, as pastoral clergy, rectors in seminaries and very often as heads of religious communities.

Today we find clandestine rings of active homosexuals and lesbians within the ranks of clergy and religious. These groups protect one another and create networks of influence, infiltrating many areas within the Church's innermost operations. These cabals are not easy to dismantle. The strategy of the Evil One is highly sophisticated. It is as if the Church is a computer network which he infects with a satanic virus. This then spreads through communities like a cancer, corrupting them from within and, ultimately, bringing about their complete destruction.

The available statistics on these movements, particularly in the United States and Canada, are very alarming indeed. This evil is so endemic in the Church today that I could devote volumes to it, but this would only give them more unwarranted publicity. It is better to redouble our prayer efforts, asking the Lord God to touch their hearts, and for the awakening of the Church to the enormity of such pervasive evil, in the hope that She will take decisive steps to stop the rot.

It can be perplexing and frustrating in the extreme for those who are brave enough to attempt to report crimes involving serious sexual impropriety to the relevant Church authority. They may receive little or no support, that is if they receive a response at all. There are countless cases of entire parishes banding together to denounce abuses and sexual misconduct only to have their grievances go unacknowledged. They may even have to suffer the pain and ignominy of having to harbor a known sexual predator whom no one is prepared to stop.

Another major satanic assault on the Church today comes from several, so-called, modern theologians, who, having fallen prey to the spirit of arrogance and spiritual pride, have subsequently formulated many dangerous heresies. There are priests of religious communities who, acting in complete defiance of God's Law, and without regard for Church authority, brazenly teach the most egregious errors. We have only to think of those proponents of Liberation Theology who preached a purely rational approach to the Gospel in their attempt to justify their Marxist worldview, ignoring the fundamentals of the Faith and subverting its transcendental, spiritual nature. We see the same hubris at work among some Scripture scholars who attempt to introduce modes of interpreting Sacred Scripture which are not consonant with the mind and heart of the Church, and which are, in fact, more in keeping with the latest gnostic discoveries. They assert that Jesus did not walk on water, that he did not multiply the loaves of bread, that Jonah was a myth, that Moses did not divide the waters and that the story of Adam and Eve is merely a fable. I have heard this from the pulpit in Latin American countries and in other parts of the Catholic world. Nowadays, the errors freely propagated by these modern-day heretics are innumerable.

Among the tremendous attacks that Satan is bringing upon the Church in our time, we must include the whole area of liturgical abuse. Today we commonly find priests celebrating completely improvised Masses to such an extent that it is distressing just being present. Great sacrileges are committed every day against the Divine Liturgy by consecrated hands, and with the greatest cynicism and indifference. We see priests who give general absolutions in weak parishes where few go to Confession. The faithful feel themselves betrayed with no one to defend their interests or to put order back into the Church. They are "harassed and helpless like sheep without a shepherd" (Matt. 9:36).

Many today come to Holy Communion in a state of mortal sin and without the least intention of changing. It is common to see couples living in *common-law*, going to Communion with the permission of the priest, who is likely to be in a worse state of sin than they are. We see Masses being celebrated for active homosexual couples who approach to receive the Holy Body of Jesus, hand-in-hand with their gay partners.

Whenever we hear individuals call for the Church to abolish the discipline of priestly celibacy, the chances are it is because they themselves are living in mortal sin. When these kinds of changes are proposed, it is a clear sign that the exponents are already soiled by the sins of impurity and are intent on dragging thousands of other souls with them to hell. Sexual immorality is a common evil, as natural as infection. It takes over one cell at a time spreading to invade neighboring cells, and, in time, the whole body. It is not because priests are unable to marry that they forsake celibacy and abandon chastity. Such individuals are fundamentally unreliable people to begin with. Had they not become priests, they would have been unfaithful spouses, unscrupulous doctors, corrupt politicians, dishonest employees, mediocre in whatever they undertook and unable to honor any lasting commitment in life on account of their unfaithful nature.

A Simple Choice

In our generation, the line separating good and evil has become very clear. We are either on God's side or Satan's - there is no gray area, as many like to think. A true Catholic is one who lives in accordance with the teachings and precepts of Catholicism, the One True Faith. The Catholic Church, founded by the Lord Jesus, stands on Sacred Tradition flowing from its Judeo-Christian roots. It is not a man-made Christianity constructed by renegade friars, apostate monarchs or 'Enlightenment' intellectuals. Ours is an authentic Christian heritage, one marked by the very wounds of Her Lord. The Catholic Church is Christ's own Mystical Body.

This is the Church that, throughout Her two-thousand-year history, has continued to forge Her way ahead, impelled as She is by the blood of the millions of Catholic martyrs who sacrificed their lives and have provided a territory of salvation for those chosen to enter the glory of the Resurrection with Christ. This Church, God's Pilgrim People, continues to journey through Her earthly exile accompanied as She is by The Lord Jesus, who is alive in the Eucharist. This wondrous Bread of Life strengthens the children of the Church who, having been purified through the sacrament of Confession, are provided with a sacramental way of salvation.

This is the Church that awaits the coming of Jesus Christ in His glory with the angels and saints, while She prepares a people chosen by God to encounter Him and to be resurrected with Him on the last day, just as the Lord promised (John. 6:40). The Church communicates to us God's own teaching, a teaching which leads humanity on the path of redemption. The Divine Revelation which the Church sets before us is a reality that must be accepted by faith. Each of us must decide whether or not he or she will believe in, and fully embrace revealed truth. Doing so means accepting the doctrine of *The Fall* and the *Original Sin* which it brought about. It also means being able to acknowledge ourselves as pilgrims on the way to the Heavenly Jerusalem.

It is a real grace to be freed from the slavery of the earthly Egypt, that is to say, the binding shackles of worldly materialism. When we are able to focus on the hope which we glimpse on the distant horizon, of a better world beyond this one, we are living a true life in the Spirit. It is a joy to make our earthly pilgrimage knowing the true happiness that awaits us when we reach our final destination, the heavenly homeland which Jesus promised from the Cross. For those who can hear the cry of *Jesus Crucified*, this is Salvation. Through His Cross and Resurrection, those of His disciples who will follow Him, who will take up their own crosses and allow themselves to be crucified with Him, are raised to new, everlasting life. In the Church today, it is plain to see the clear line that divides the merely cultural Catholics from those who live their lives in the heart of the Cross.

The first group, the cultural Catholics, have no sense of the mystical, no understanding of Christ as an eternal spiritual presence in their lives. They go to Christ only for their material needs. Despite knowing the fullness of the truth, these individuals are far from embracing the spirit of this truth at its core. They are the modern descendants of the Pharisees of Jesus' time, a people of hardened hearts, who claim to be of God by fulfilling the law and its precepts, but who are, in reality, far from living it in its spirit, in true love and spiritual poverty.

There is nothing more sad or more disheartening for a Catholic than to encounter worldly priests who are purely rational and completely lacking a sense of the spiritual. They are like magnificent ships anchored in the port, whose sails will never again be unfurled in the high seas of the Spirit, ships that will never set sail to reach its port of destination. We can perceive their frustration, even if they appear upbeat at times. More often, we sense, through the veil, the great misery residing in their moribund souls. Many will seek respite from their spiritual paralysis in intellectual pursuits, constructing their own, alternative vision of 'the truth' revealed by Our Lord Jesus in the Gospel. Through these 'clever', progressive theologies they become even more puffed up, falling prey to the demonic spirit of pride.

During our own times of battle against the demons of indifference and pride, our duty, as children of God, then, is to strengthen our Christian witness by imitating the humility and the spiritual poverty of our Lord. It is enough just to be courageous, to fully embrace the cross, and to live the truth, just as it was revealed by Our Lord, without omission or compromise.

It is vital that a true Catholic be prepared to fight against the forces of darkness; forces that beset the path of God's pilgrim people with all sorts of snares and pitfalls. Since our struggle is against fallen angels who are swifter than we can imagine, effective combat requires us to strengthen ourselves through fidelity to God.

By presenting this vision of the Church, it is not my intent to preach a fatalistic message of despair. What I highlight describes the current situation throughout virtually the entire world today. But, we must always keep in mind that, while the situation is lamentable, the Church has had these elements from the beginning. Such is the nature of the battle. Today, however, because we are closer than ever to the Lord's return, the battle against the enemy of souls grows evermore intense because the devil knows his time is running out. (Rev. 12:12)

The reader should be aware that my presentation here is intentionally couched in a spiritual language. It is not my purpose to set forth a sort of political theology or liberal conception of religion. I am speaking in terms of a mystical reign, a reign that those beguiled by the world will find impossible to grasp. For these, such talk is delusional madness. The very suggestion of any other, deeper reality would be deemed by them to be a dangerous fiction, and those proposing or representing such a thing would be considered a menace to society, a threat to be eliminated. But we should remember, it was ever thus. Throughout history, the prophets who spoke of God's Kingdom, a world that seemed so very different to our own, were put to death. Chief among these, of course, was Our Lord, the one we seek to follow.

The world has always been the same. It is like the Egypt of the Exodus, the place where man seeks to thrive and flourish without the God who is his source. In his arrogance, man even seeks to reign on earth, usurping God who is the One True King. In this way man's existence becomes illusory, opposing, as it does, objective reality. Nothing in the world to-day should surprise us, then. It is just more of the same. It is the world that Abraham left behind in Babylon; the same world Moses inhabited and where Solomon built the Temple of God. It is the world that crucified the Lord Jesus and that today is imbued by a culture of death.

The Authority of the People of God

How can we, as laity, find our role within the Church's mission today? This question is of paramount importance for Catholics nowadays because we continue to be part of an overly-clerical Church. Down through the centuries, this Church has often confronted the empire of the Evil One, but without adequately involving the laity, whose vast ranks have gone largely unexploited. Today, sadly, the bitter fruits of such an over-clericalized Church are all too plain to see. One of the gravest consequences of this sad phenomenon is the so-called Protestant Reformation and, since then and flowing from this 'Reformation', the seductive allure that these alternative Christian groups, or sects, often hold for the Catholic lay faithful. Once the 'Reformation' opened the door to the defiance of the Sacred Tradition, the enormous chasm created between the clergy and the laity meant that the latter soon became easy prey for dissident, apostate sects. Many of the Catholics recruited by sects and New Age movements are those who have become bitterly disillusioned with today's clergy and religious communities, often feeling themselves to be excluded or overlooked as valued members of the Church.

Today, more than ever, we are called to be united as a Church and to become more fully aware of our true identity in Christ; an identity which the *Scriptures* reveal to us. Just as the angels of God form a hierarchy, so must the militant Church. Hierarchies do not correspond to levels of importance before God, or creatures. They constitute, rather, levels of responsibility in the spiritual battle for the defense of souls. They should reflect, for example, who is most capable of loving and forgiving or who is able to follow the Divine Master most perfectly.

Herein lies the real challenge of the Catholic Faith and the necessary requirement of an effective soldier in the army of the Lord. To be a true child of God, and of His Church, means understanding that our particular rank or position becomes irrelevant once we join the battle. What matters is that we are well-armed and properly trained; that we are ready to fight to win the souls which God has entrusted to us. It matters not whether I am a bishop or a priest, a nun or a monk, or a simple layman going about his business in the world. What matters is my fidelity to God and to His Church. This is what makes us truly brothers and sisters of the Lord. (Matt. 12:49).

In the main, the Church continues to be too clerical. The most common attempt to reconcile the disparity is to clericalize the laity, inviting them to become extraordinary ministers of the Eucharist, readers of the Word or other types of clerical ministry, so as to have the laity sharing the service of the altar with the ordained ministers. This is not what the Church needs in these times. If She is to engage more effectively in the mission given to Her by the Lord, we need to establish a clear bridge between clergy and laity, each in their own role, with their own particular responsibilities and charisms.

Why, we might ask, are Evangelical and Pentecostal sects continuing to spread, especially in the Far East? This is simply because people find in them a welcoming place where they encounter human warmth, and where their emotions and struggles to survive are recognized and attended to. In the

Catholic Church, not enough clergy are have 'come down from the altar' to embrace the congregation, to permit the faithful to speak, or allow the Holy Spirit to speak to His people through the mouth of the humble and the simple. What is more, the Holy Spirit has been held captive by the unyielding bars of clerical pretentiousness.

We are facing a great battle in our times because the deeper humanity falls into sin, the more evil are the spirits that emerge into the world from the abyss. Never before has humanity fallen so low and never before have such enormous giants of hell been loosed on the world. If we continue as we are, the world will become so horrible that it will be unbearable. If God had not promised to shorten this time of tribulation out of compassion for His faithful, even the most loyal souls would not prevail.

It is very sad to see those whom God has called to look after His sheep – his priests and religious – so completely seduced by the world. Without proper shepherds, what will become of the flock?, we may ask. The Catholic family, too, is in grave danger today. Many have fallen into the abyss and will drag down many generations to come, because the harm they are doing to themselves by neglecting God is so great, that they will spiritually blind and deafen their children; effectively robbing them of all the graces they should have inherited from God.

The engagement of today's Catholics in politics, the economy, and science and culture in general, is one of complete mediocrity in spiritual terms. The need to be politically correct and to protect one's image and interests is the priority. The spiritual battle, where the life, morality and spiritual integrity of the people of God are to be defended, has been all but abandoned. Every Catholic, regardless of his vocation or position in the Church, has a territory of souls to defend. If he does not defend them, they will be affected by the demons from the depths of hell who will seek to destroy them.

These demons have complete contempt for us and ultimately seek our eternal death. They know every detail of our efforts against them. They begin their attacks against Catholics with exactly the same temptation with which Satan tempted Jesus in the desert; "All these I will give you, if you will fall down and worship me" (Matt. 4:9). One of the greatest trials that a Catholic faces is resisting the seduction of material riches. If the devil fails to buy him with money, he will try to buy him with social, political or religious power, and if this fails, then through terrible vices. If we are strictly disciplined within the lines of the Faith in a religious or priestly life, he will attempt to trap us, perverting this discipline and converting it into activism, overpowering us with a thirst for knowledge and religious power. When we understand how astonishing are the evil forces ranged against us and that our eternal destiny is at stake, we begin to realize how terrible is the danger facing those souls who have lost the fear of God.

We have been created truly free, but this freedom must be used in the right way if we are to realize our 'redemption in Christ'. We must use our freedom, waken up and take our proper place in the spiritual battle - sounding the trumpet, keeping everyone alert - so that we are able to more effectively guard the territory of the souls entrusted to us by the Lord.

The Ecclesiastical Hierarchy

In this book, I have mentioned many times "the territory of the souls that have been entrusted to us." I have done so intentionally, and will probably do so again, because the fact is, our whole life as Catholics has to do with souls. Not just our own soul, but those of the millions upon millions of human beings whom we are able to nourish during the short time of our earthly pilgrimage. We can all be witnesses of holiness, as true instruments of God's perfect plan. By humbling ourselves, we are able to fulfill our life's mission and the Lord is able to do great things through our ordinary, seemingly insignificant, little lives. God uses us lowly, wretched creatures, to carry out such magnificent works. If only we could really grasp this, how happy we would be. We would desire nothing more than to belong to God, to be His instruments and to be filled with the deep joy that this brings. As Catholics, we must pray for God to open our eyes fully to the mystery of the Faith. If we could glimpse the true reality of this Faith, even for a moment, we would fall to our knees in ceaseless adoration and total self-offering to God in thanksgiving for so great a gift.

In order to understand the authority of the Church, it is helpful to reflect on the Scripture passage wherein Saint Luke describes Paul's journey to Jerusalem where he meets with the pillars of the Church, Peter, James and John. As Scripture recounts, they found no error in Paul's teachings, nor had they anything new to teach him. After laying their hands on him, the apostles sent Paul out to preach to the Gentiles. Their only specific recommendation was that he should have concern for the poor (Gal. 2:9-10).

By going to see the apostles in Jerusalem in this way, Paul, led by the Holy Spirit, is acknowledging them as the legitimate leaders of the Church. This illustrates for us the ecclesiastical hierarchy Jesus established in the nascent Church. Paul co-operates with this established order in perfect obedience. He could easily have started the first Christian sect, one independent of the hierarchy. He had seen the Lord, after all. During his encounter with Jesus on the road to Damascus, Saul was infused with wisdom, the same grace which the apostles received during the three years of Jesus' public life, grace that was confirmed and activated by the Paraclete at Pentecost. Saint Paul, however, submitted himself to the older apostles, with much humility, and accepted their instructions to go and to preach to the Gentiles.

The vital element of obedience within the Church rests on an understanding of the Mystical Body of Christ as the true reality of our Faith. When we understand our Church as essentially a mystical reality, a true kingdom that is not of this world, one that can be entered only through the Cross, we become aware of our nature and responsibility as Christians. When we fully understand these dimensions of our Faith, we are ready to embrace supernatural life and become transformed. No longer is our natural way of living based solely on our human nature. It becomes focused entirely on God. There follows a real sense of direction; the Gospel comes to life; it becomes a real support and guide in all our daily striving.

Awakening to a true Christian life at this level makes it easier to understand the authority of the militant Church. Without a mystical conception of the Faith, we will never be able to submit to the authority of the Church or follow the guidance of the Pope, the bishops or our parish priest. When we are fully aware of this authority, however, we will obey with a joy and docility of heart and follow the teachings and guidance of the Holy Father, bringing many blessings to the whole Church.

If we are to cultivate an attitude of compassion and charity towards all Catholics, clerics, religious and laity, it is important that we accept the limitations and sinful nature of the Church's humanity. Only in this way will we be able to unite ourselves to, and fully participate in, pastoral and diocesan missionary activity and attain a richer life in the spirit. Obedience, from the point of view of the authority of the Church, has to do with the simple fact of recognizing the Church as spiritual mother, as a cradle of the soul, as an oasis of our pilgrimaging, as the guide, compass and map to our *Eternal Homeland.*

Many Catholics are now far from the Church because of the shameful behavior of some members of the Church. This means, of course, that their belonging to the Church has depended on purely human factors. This is a grave shortcoming but something which is sadly all too common among the faithful and particularly prevalent when it comes to people's relationship to clergy. To be able to see beyond the veil of human nature, and to grasp the depth of the mystical presence and authority of Jesus in the Church, requires spiritual maturity. Only then are we able to overcome those human factors, such as our dislike of the priest's personality, which might present something of a spiritual obstacle for us. This spiritual maturity provides the necessary platform from which to launch ourselves into the realm of the Spirit, the only real and lasting strength and support in our earthly battle.

When we have difficulties with obedience on account of the conduct of others, it is a sure sign that we are incapable of transcending the realm of human nature to give the lordship to Jesus as Master and Lord of the Church. So that we might learn to obey His will, God journeys with us through the centuries with a consistent and firm pedagogy. He cast Adam and Eve out of Paradise as soon as they disobeyed, and told them what they must do without the privilege of His presence. He cursed the serpent and also the ground or dust from which He created it, but He did not curse Adam and Eve. He punished them by making them live a new reality without the privileges of Paradise. God taught Cain the consequences of the sin of having killed his own brother. He banished him from the midst of his family, but did not deprive him of the means to survive. Because of his sin, Cain was separated from the rest and sent into exile, but God also placed His protective mark on Cain so that no one would kill him (Gen. 4:13-16).

In the interaction between God and Cain we see that, despite man's expulsion from Paradise, God continued to be close to Adam and Eve's first children, speaking to them and counselling them. However, the evil of sin had already nested in their hearts during their exile, and that sin led to an ever more profound exile and distancing from God, heaping countless curses on generations who would be estranged from God for centuries.

God teaches humanity the unconditional way of obedience through Abel's actions. He shows us clearly how fidelity to the good exposes us to the enemy, but only with regard to what is mortal and temporal. Despite Abel's goodness, we see he is destroyed by the envy and violence of his brother. This is the most complicated and fearful reality for those who are baptized in Christ and who, therefore, have true knowledge of the Spirit. They must learn to give up their attachment to their earthly dwelling, including their own natural life. If one is to follow in Abel's steps, one must live with an awareness that he is a pilgrim who is being constantly tested in love and, therefore, in obedience - the very virtues violated by *Original Sin*.

The lesson of Cain and Abel is a great teaching of God which shows us how to return to the original state in which He created us. God has given us free will, but, at the same time, He is always expressing his own Divine Will very clearly to us. This is so we might become wise in all our decisions and not get lost on our way home to Our Father's House. This means submitting to God, just as Abel did when he bowed before Him and chose to put God's Will before his own. God does not watch us from afar in order to judge our actions. He is always willing to rescue us from our bad choices. We exist at all times under His merciful pedagogy. We now have the blessing of the Eucharist as our true nourishment and spiritual sustenance. Despite our sin and unfaithfulness, God offers us the way of reconciliation and strength. By means of the Bread of Eternal Life, we are able to overcome our evil inclinations.

Throughout our sacred history, we see very clearly that God has never abandoned us. Although we have been exiled from the original Paradise, He has always walked beside us. Today, thanks to the sacraments, we are able to grasp the mysteries of God's pedagogy in our lives and consciously conform to His Will by means of the strength we gain from the Eucharist and the grace that flows from obeying His commandments. We are also inspired by God to take this treasure to the many souls living in the darkness of this exile, who do not know God's love and who have never lived in the light.

Despite our exile, God has made Himself present among us in the most wonderful way. He remains with us in our sufferings, in our inability to recognize Him, in our laziness and indifference to the sacred, in our failure to decide to be good. He knows what we have become, and has walked with us through hundreds of generations, patiently showing us how we should behave and what we must do to regain His friendship. He has forgiven us and forgotten all the evil we have committed against Him since Adam and Eve's expulsion from Paradise. After so many years and such precious lessons, warnings and punishments, God moves, through the person of His Son, and appears to us again, speaking to each one of us once more, just as He did to our parents in the Garden of Eden before the *Fall*. He knew we would be incapable of obeying Him by ourselves because we carried the grave wound of sin. Only God's mercy and forgiveness could restore, heal and redeem us.

He descended from on high and came down to the Kingdom of death, imperfection and chaos. He embraced each of us personally, no longer speaking to us from the burning bush, or appearing in thunder and lightning, or sending messengers to warn us. He made Himself perfectly present, becoming one of us, being temporarily inferior to the angels (Heb. 2:9). Despite all this, many of us are still incapable of relating to the Man-God of the Gospel or recognizing Him as the true God. There are some who persist in a state of sin with no fear of God, even when the truth has been revealed to them and the Holy Spirit has rested in their hearts in Baptism. We must strive, with the help of Our Lord Jesus, to emerge from the Egypt of our earthly life because, without His help, we would simply be unable to do so.

The present state of the Church may be lamentable, but it has always been thus. It is no different from the times when Cain and Abel made their respective offerings. It is the same today as when the treachery of Judas co-existed alongside the unswerving fidelity of Saint John. At the time of Jesus' priestly self-sacrifice, the Jewish priesthood had become corrupted by the spiritual arrogance and pride of God's Chosen People. Good and evil, the wheat and the darnel, have always grown up side by side in the desert. Until the Kingdom of Death comes to pass, this will always be an inescapable reality. It is imperative that we know exactly where Egypt is in relation to our own spiritual journey. When we understand that this life is an earthly pilgrimage in the desert, we are able to see true life more clearly. We are better able to keep our gaze fixed on the horizon of our *Eternal Homeland* where we will live happily ever after with God.

Guardian of the Truth

The Catholic Church is the *Barque of Peter* making her pilgrim voyage on earth. She is an oasis where souls find spiritual sustenance during the earthly exile that they must endure on their way to eternal glory. She is also a sure guide. The proper interpretation of the Sacred Scriptures is a matter of the greatest importance and God has given His Church, that is the Catholic Church, the special grace of infallibly interpreting His Holy Word. Because she is illumined and sanctified by the Holy Spirit, the Church is both wise and holy.

Our entire spiritual warfare can be said to be centered in God's revealed truth, Divine Revelation. Each word that comes from God has a devastating effect on the forces of evil. No creature of darkness can withstand the sound of the Word. It is indeed a great responsibility to read and proclaim the Word of God, but unfortunately, this is something that many fail to appreciate.

If we are to properly understand Divine Revelation, it is imperative that we consider the entire sweep of Judeo-Christian history, which is the history of salvation itself. Through the centuries, the Scriptures have been tampered with and manipulated by numerous unscrupulous individuals and biblical sects, intent on propagating all sorts of false doctrines. Their efforts have resulted in an erosion of the genuine sacramental precepts which Jesus taught.

Lacking direction from Mother Church, the Bible has been mishandled and this has resulted in mediocre translations which are susceptible to wrong interpretation. This, in turn, has led to the creation of countless pseudo-Christian sects operating in the world, without proper discernment, under the guidance of dubious translations, or versions, of the Bible. Today, we observe with sadness how the Word of God has become a Bible-based Christian cult, which proclaims an earthly paradise and promotes only temporal human interests, instead of that of Christ, whose Holy Name they take in vain.

The commercialization of Jesus' name, through pseudo-Christian sects and biblical schools, has given rise to an emotional Christianity, which proposes to millions a false presentation of God's Word. The counterfeit gospel peddled by this hybrid Christianity is, in fact, a rejection of the Cross. It promises physical health and prosperity and an end to suffering and demands little of its adherents, declaring, 'Jesus has already paid for us all! Alleluia!' It is not that people are naive, but they do possess a sort of innate tendency for superstition and a weakness for magic and prognostication. Presenting these to people in the name of Jesus gives their leaders an air of legitimacy and religious respectability and makes what is being peddled seem all the more appealing.

Many supposedly Christian movements are, in reality, sects allied to those whose true agenda is the establishment of a *New World Order* with a *One-world Government.* By completely eradicating all religion, they seek, largely through the promotion of abortion and homosexualism, to control the world's population. Gradually these sects have gone from being denominational to nondenominational. While continuing to masquerade as Christians, they have become increasingly conformed to, and suffused by, the malevolent spirit of the New Age, from whence they draw their true inspiration. These false Christians promote causes and agendas that are manifestly opposed to God's Holy Will, as He reveals it to us through His Word. So-called gay 'marriage' is one such cause. 'Marriage' between homosexuals is a plan of satanic origin, intentionally devised to eliminate the gift of procreation and to destroy the family, as God constituted it. This diabolical scheme opposes the Law of God and directly affects the *economy of salvation*, which is closely tied to procreation, the generation of human beings.

We are engaged in a spiritual battle with potentially cataclysmic consequences. Evil uses our culture, society, technological advancements and, in particular, the globalization of arts, music and literature, to pervert humanity with its own creativity. It is not that civilization as such is satanic, rather that evil is corrupting much of what God inspires in us by His Spirit. Evil's most effective strategy for conquering territory is to create division. God does not divide; He is unity and love. Where there is division, there is a demon. If we recognize where our enemy is, we will then become more effective in our goals and focused on the right things. By dividing the Catholic Church, evil intends to manipulate the conscience of believers who have no-one to defend them. These same forces of division and confusion are making great gains today in the traditionally Catholic countries of Europe, such as Ireland, France, Spain and Portugal, among others.

The world will continue to be as it is while the Kingdom of Death persists. We are in the school of souls and we must understand clearly the nature of our pilgrimage on earth. Because of *Original Sin*, our human nature is not satisfied with the truth revealed by God, and even resists it. Without a personal spiritual experience with the revealed Word, and proper consideration and respect for *Sacred Tradition*, our religion becomes subject to rationalism and remains merely human. This is the intellectual conception of the Faith that is held by so many modern theologians whose ideas have been the source of so much heresy and the cause of so much apostasy.

The Church is not merely another biblical school like those of modern Christianity or Protestant sects. She is a solicitous Mother anointed with the Truth from on high. The Church has been given the power to impart this truth to souls in a simple language, through a catechesis inspired by the living Spirit of God who resides in the heart of the Eucharistic tabernacle. From there, the Spirit radiates, through the Divine Liturgy, knowledge of all that was revealed by Jesus in The Word. This is accomplished with simplicity, humility and love of the Father, who presents Himself in the sacrifice of His Son and makes Himself available to souls by sacramental means.

We can see in the Scriptures how the people of God were sent into exile for centuries and handed over to pagan powers that profaned the sacredness of the Temple of God, as we see with King Nebuchadnezzar and his sons in the Book of Daniel. Things have not changed much. God continues teaching us through a strict and firm pedagogy. He will continue to do so until Jesus returns and the powers of hell are permanently subjugated beneath His feet and the sting of death no longer holds power over the people of God.

The Enemy Within

How can we respond to the evil *Spirit of Division* assailing the Church while remaining calm, just and charitable towards those who have been seduced by the illusions of a hybrid Christianity? The New Age movements have now become active evangelizers of believers' own families and friends, enticing them into sects and exposing them to all sorts of dangerous ideologies and philosophies. We are once again in the Ephesus of Saint Paul where hearts seek signs and miracles. We must re-evangelize our Church in the spirit of Saint Paul, exhorting all denominations to unite once again into One Body. We must call them to look beyond mere earthly goods and to begin to invest in their spiritual economy. We have to protect the people of God from the allure of the *Prosperity Gospel* whose attraction is only going to increase with the passing of time.

Jesus foretold these events. He predicted that even believers would be deceived by the prodigies that Satan would carry out in the name of God. As the true Church of Christ, united in grace, we must fight the good fight of the Gospel, understanding that we are facing a particular spiritual landscape that calls for both decisive action and careful discernment. The Enemy adapts himself according to each situation, subtly exerting his malevolent influence from the shadows. With each generation, he insinuates himself anew, using tried and tested tactics to ensnare souls.

Many modern theologians and liberal clergy, as they are known today, take great pains to ignore Saint Paul, because the Apostle's teaching directly challenges the dearly held philosophies and ideologies of the materialistic culture that they serve. In the conduct of their pastoral duties. It is not God's Law or the fear of the Lord that concerns them, but human respect and being popular with the people. This is why Saint Paul is a threat to them. To live a Pauline priesthood means risking the loss of people's support, including their financial support. Several priests have told me that this fear is paralyzing for many within the Church. It is commonplace for priests to be more concerned with pleasing people than pleasing God. They are often so worried about their reputation, and their image, that they are even prepared to compromise the message of the Gospel.

In every time and place, Saint Paul's message is a powerful weapon for combating evil. It will remain thus until the end of time. As my apostolate has unfolded over the years, I have come to realize that most Catholic faithful want to hear the truth; they appreciate being exhorted. This does not necessarily mean that they will go out to make a radical change in their lives - many leave sad, just like the rich young man in the Gospel - but they recognize when they have been given the truth or shown the true way.

I have had the same experience with Catholic young people in many countries. They are perfectly receptive to pure, undiluted truth, to the spirit of Saint Paul's challenging words. In today's world, immersed in a New Age culture with all sorts of superstition, occult practices and pagan philosophies, it is not surprising to see our young people being seduced by all sorts of temptation, through fashion, the media and music. They are largely unaware of the grave spiritual dangers they are being exposed to, including suicide and other evils. There are families whose children have had encounters with Satan after they joined a satanic church on the Internet. They became enslaved by suicidal thoughts and feelings, as can happen to youngsters who get involved with certain youth cults, such as 'Emos', for instance. Through these channels, children may infest their homes and families with legions of spirits and begin to experience demonic manifestations.

How can we possibly stand idly by, while the Church remains fast asleep and in the face of such spiritual peril? Serious questions need to be asked when we see a Catholic flock without an exorcist. Why would a bishop refuse to appoint an exorcist in his diocese? Is it because of the poor formation he received in the seminary, ignorance of basic demonology, or simply a rejection of the possibility of supernatural events? Is it because of a very 'rational' conception or a psychologizing of demonic manifestations?

The Catholic Church is not a corporation, or a social club, or a human rights movement. It is not a registered charity or an NGO (Non-Governmental Organization). Priesthood and religious life are not just professions; they are sacred vocations, a direct calling from God. We have a Church today in which it is very common to find clergy who are absolutely ignorant and indifferent to the spiritual world. One wonders what they are even doing in the Church.

Now is not the time to keep silent or abandon our post. The sheep are being left defenseless, with no shepherds to protect them. We must denounce those in leadership positions in the Church who have forsaken their sacred duty. Our exhortations may not be well received by some bishops but urgent change must be pursued regardless. Whenever there is some kind of review or investigation, it is only the dishonest who have something to fear. The one who is faithful is never offended. On the contrary, he will assist the effort and make himself part of the solution. This is true both within and outside the Church. In general, opposition to such change comes from those who are living sinful lives. Their reactions, when confronted or faced with investigation, often betrays them and make our efforts to expose them that much easier.

Sincere and honest Catholics understand that urgent change is needed and that it is up to all of us to act. Any criticism, of course, must always be made respectfully and in humble submission to Church authority, but our voices must be heard. Our Church needs true Catholics to defend Her. So, let us imitate Christ, let us not be afraid to fight for truth. We must battle bravely now in the struggle for the purification of the Church, for if we do not, the enemy will surely continue to undermine us from within.

The Limitations of Reason

So many Catholic hearts today have become hardened by materialism and rationalism. In our world, reason has been elevated to an almost divine standing. Although reason is a most precious gift from God, when it is not centered on the love of God and is not harmoniously in balance with faith, it can easily blind us with pride and self-love. This opens the door to a spirit of self-sufficiency, centered on the search for self-esteem and personal fulfillment, a quest that, in reality, precludes the Cross. This is very dangerous spiritually because the Cross of Christ is, or ought to be, at the center of our Christian life.

We can forget sometimes just how limited human reason is. It cannot inform us about events of the past, for example, or about what is in the mind of another. Reason only knows what has been revealed to it. Consider, for instance, the following questions: What is the purpose of our existence? Why did God create man? What is the nature of the next life? What was in God's mind when He created man? We can only know the answer to these deep mysteries if God Himself reveals them to us. We need God's revelation to help us to understand the meaning and purpose of our lives. Otherwise our entire existence becomes meaningless and futile. It is through the Revealed Word that we have come to know that Christ founded

His Church and that, in and through the Church, God Himself is with us.

We know that God protects His Church from false teachings and gives His faithful children the necessary discernment to be able to recognize when evil is being preached and promoted, even when the error emanates from His own priests. It is our duty to be on our guard against such dangers, remaining vigilant, and taking care to ensure that our attitude to the sins of the Church is more than just a passive one. When called for, we must also be prepared to take action to stand against it. Such evil is not acceptable to the people of God. It is better to lose the support of those who are unfaithful than to fail God through the sin of omission.

Naturally, the issues addressed here must be broached with charity and sensitivity. We do not seek conflict, but, should it come, we will not allow it to distract us from our primary goal which is to present the purity of the truth without compromise. We are preparing to effect the change that is so desperately needed in the Church and in the world today. So much has happened in the last hundred years to undermine the Faith and confound the faithful that they have become greatly confused and rendered powerless to do anything about it.

The people of God have been taken by surprise. In the span of just one century, things have progressed materially, so far and so fast, that men have not been able to keep themselves sufficiently spiritually vigilant, or discern from among so many changes, the good from the bad. Bedazzled by human science, technology and industrialization, the human family has slipped into a sort of spiritual *coma*. The Church has slumbered while the dark forces of her *Enemy* have continued to work without ceasing. Now, as the Church is finally beginning to wake, she finds millions of emaciated souls, totally enchanted by the materialism surrounding them and beguiled by all sorts of illusions.

The Church's battle against evil in our times, however, is no different from what She has faced before. It has never been otherwise. It is only the spiritual cycles and seasons that change, and God alone knows how these work. We do know, however, from Divine Revelation, that, with the passing of time, we draw ever closer to the return of the Lord Jesus and that the battle will become more and more fierce as we approach the end. At the same time, we also know that God will always ensure that His soldiers are properly equipped and prepared for the battle they must face during their pilgrimage on earth.

There is no need to be afraid. No, this awareness strengthens us, as 'we wait in joyful hope'. Knowing that God works in such close collaboration with us is what gives us confidence to fight with courage and faith. God has made known His friendship and love for humanity from the first days of our exile. His kindness and forgiveness were already manifested in the compassionate way in which He treated Cain, who had sinned so grievously. We, in our turn, must also embrace friendship with God and be faithful to Him. God is on our side and no force of nature, no creature, no circumstance of our material existence will ever be able to disrupt the flow of His friendship to us.

No, we have nothing to fear. The Church needs us to always remember that Jesus is truly alive in the Eucharist. If the faithful are unaware, disinterested and indifferent, we must testify, no matter what they say or think, that it is really and truly God Whom we receive at Mass and Whom we visit in the Most Blessed Sacrament. There is nothing more sacred or more important to defend. If our parish priest has been poorly trained and contaminated in the seminary by false theologies, he may not believe in the Real Presence. If he is preaching these errors from the pulpit, we need to take immediate action and go to speak with him directly. We cannot ignore the gross abuse and maltreatment of our Church by the arrogance and religious pride of today's Pharisees. These are not the times for people-pleasing or being afraid of what they might think of us. Our Church is falling into a devastating Protestantism which we have a grave responsibility to do all in our power to prevent.

What will become of our traditions? At the rate we are going today, one wonders if anything will remain of Sacred Tradition, when 'Christianity' is being spread by magicians and salesmen who have turned it into an industry, that proclaims a Jesus without the Cross, without sacrifice. It is important to remember how the Divine Liturgy began. Abraham offered a sacrifice to God, as well as a tithe to the priest, Melchizedek. This meeting established the basis of a priestly tradition, which will continue to be an integral part of life on earth until the Lord returns. Doing away with our Sacred Liturgy would be like trying to live without breathing. The people of God have been given a Church, which is God's army on earth. It is here to stay. It is the rock on which faithful Catholics ground themselves, on which they stand firm to fight the good fight of the Gospel, in fulfillment of the Church's mission to save souls for God's Kingdom.

The sky may appear gloomy at times, but God will always be behind the clouds of this vale of tears, waiting for us, to help us carry our crosses each day, until we finally reach the summit of Golgotha. We have been given the map and the compass. We have been shown the way to our eternal abode with the Father, who never leaves us alone, not even for a minute. We can draw great solace from knowing the revealed truth, the Spirit of God is with us always, even to the end of time.

Life After Life

It is extraordinary to be able to live this earthly life knowing that we are God's children and that our lives do not end in a cold grave but 'happily ever after' with our Father, in Paradise. Such knowledge helps us to withstand the fearful moment of death and brings with it relief, and soothing strength, to a poor and afflicted mortality which naturally dreads the gradual, relentless and painful decline unto death.

God has given us the hope of eternal life through his own Son's flesh and blood. This *Pledge of our Salvation* strengthens our souls and gives us the assurance of our immortality in Him. In this way, we are able to transcend our temporal nature. How great it is to be alive knowing that life is truly eternal, that we are immortal! We feel safe and secure in the knowledge that we live a life that will never end; a glory where there will be no more tears, no more death. There is an enormous difference between one who has received this grace of eternal life in Jesus Christ and consciously lives it to the full, and the one who, despite having received it, still lives as a mere mortal, plagued by torments, their own limitations and the fear of death, consumed by all sorts of worldly concerns.

We are called to share the gift of the faith we have received with the souls that have been entrusted to us, that is to say, with everyone around us, without exception. We have a duty to transmit the Faith that we have inherited from our ancestors, unconditionally. Faith is not just a gift. It is responsibility that presses on us to be passed on. The faith dwelling in us has been infused into our hearts by God through the sacrament of Baptism. It springs forth from within us, in all we do. If we are not faithful to God, our faith is dormant, and inactive, useless. But, if we are faithful, our faith breaks forth like a healing light, bringing hope and peace to all those we encounter. Faith is the presence of the Holy Spirit living in the heart of those who love and obey God.

Sadly, the faith of many today has become terribly weak, with very few exceptions (perhaps in the Eastern rites). The Church worldwide has fallen prey to social, economic and political activism. For many, religion is completely superficial, a cult of men who are concerned with worldly affairs, where God has been relegated to second place. Here, the mystical is nowhere to be found and we are no longer a truly spiritual Church. The Most Blessed Sacrament has been abandoned, put to one side. Across the world, Jesus is alone and abandoned in the Eucharist. It is heartbreaking to see so many abandoned tabernacles in parishes, religious communities, seminaries and lay institutions. We fail to grasp the gravity of the responsibility entrusted to us, to keep watch with the Lord in the tabernacle, that *Holy of Holies*.

It is common today to witness great sacrileges being committed in local parishes in the daily celebration of Holy Mass. The most abominable violations of the Divine Liturgy take place everywhere, with a cold cynicism which indicates that they can only come from the spirit of evil. It would be impossible for me to share, even in several books, what I have seen mystically regarding the abuses of the Most Blessed Sacrament, and the fate of many sacerdotal souls and Catholic faithful in various states of life in the Church.

During the funeral service of someone I knew, I heard a Protestant pastor assert, in the presence of the deceased's family and friends, that his soul had gone straight to heaven. But I knew that that soul was tormented and begging for help and prayer. I was also given to know that, in all probability, this poor soul would have no-one to pray for him. This is the reality of many Christians today, even Catholics, who languish, forgotten and not prayed for in Purgatory.

Obedience

If all humanity could glimpse the spiritual world for just an instant, how different our world would be. God has a mysterious pedagogy with each soul and this earthly life is only the first part of our eternal journey, a journey that will never end. At this stage, although we may lack full knowledge or a clear vision of the hereafter, God does have a plan. Earthly life is His school for souls and we are here to learn important lessons. Each unique life has its own particular purpose, and, in keeping with the mysterious plan of Divine Will, God reveals to each soul what he or she is to understand. Here we may profitably recall Jesus' words to Saint Thomas, *"Blessed are those who have not seen and yet believe"*, (John. 20:29).

The First Commandment is unequivocal. It concerns what God demands of us regarding the spiritual world and makes clear that there are things that we are not to seek to know. Attempting to consult the dead by *spiritualism*, is one such example. We know from Sacred Scripture that, 'Anyone who does such things is an abomination to the Lord', (Deut. 18:10). So, we must not meddle with those things that God does not wish us to know. It is vital for a Christian to understand the sacredness of the spiritual world and of what is, as yet, invisible to us. We only explore such matters deeply when God expressly directs our spiritual consciousness to the Kingdom of the Spirit. Only God may order this, for it is His preserve and His alone. Satan tries to persuade us that eating of this forbidden fruit is harmless. He tempts us to dabble in magic, superstition, the occult and fortune telling and to seek knowledge of the spiritual world which God has forbidden. The consequences for those who succumb to such temptations are usually devastating.

We are called to receive the light of the Gospel without hesitation or doubts and to give our all for the salvation of souls. We are to make a quantum leap of faith and not look back. We must become Catholics who honor the Church by living in complete obedience to Her and in accordance with Her precepts. We must obey the Church just as one obeys a good and just mother because the Catholic Church is our mother. The only way to live this life in the midst of the civilization of death, which surrounds us, is by being united to the Mystical Body of Jesus which is the Church Herself.

The spiritual war in which we are embroiled as Catholics is based strategically on obedience to the *Deposit of the Faith*. There is simply no other way to combat the *Enemy of Souls*. The most effective way to discern who is on the side of light among the 'faithful' is to observe an individual's level of obedience to the Church. A member of the Church, whether clergy, religious or lay, who is not in obedience to the hierarchy is someone who is not to be trusted, or followed. One of the most obvious indicators associated with the errors and, indeed, the crimes that have sullied the Church in recent times, is disobedience. In general, this type of disobedience is the sign of a heart corrupted by sin and characterizes those souls who are in mortal peril of eternal damnation. Their hearts have become stones and their relationship with God has been hardened by pride, that great domain of evil. One cannot honestly claim to be a child of God while living a life in mortal sin. This has never been, and never will be, possible.

The times in which we are living and the events we see around us speak volumes about the wickedness in which humanity is now mired. This is why, every day, the sin against children grows greater and the crime of pedophilia is becoming more and more commonplace. This sin calls down the wrath of God on the world. Humanity has returned once again to the depraved times of Sodom and Gomorrah. If an angel of the Lord were to appear among us today, people would most likely try to pervert him.

The main reason why people lose the fear of God, and blithely fall into these sins, is their ignorance of what awaits us at the end of this life. There is an unwillingness, or an inability, to look beyond the present horizon, towards the eternal pastures, and to consider what life after life really means. Consequently, they fall prey to the Seducer who beguiles souls and persuades them to worship the things of the world.

Some, on reading these lines, may start to wonder if all hope is lost. In truth, it is actually the opposite. The salvation of souls is God's highest priority. It is our task, our mission and our duty as Catholics to spend our days on earth leading humanity to Jesus. It is not hard to see how a weak soul can get seduced by this glittering, material world. It is so easy for us to become attached to creation, human affection, material possessions, education and traditions, the pleasures of the flesh, sensuality. Boundless are the wishes and desires of the human heart.

This is precisely why it has become so urgent to fight for souls, those who are spiritually weak and centered only on the material. Many souls are in grave danger of being lost for eternity. Our duty, then, is to call humanity to wake up and to go beyond their senses and instincts and begin to reflect on how serious the matter of our eternal destiny really is. We must try to make them realize that there is much more to reality than just what the eyes can see. We need to let them know that we, human beings, are facing an eternal reality which is determined in this life. We need to remind our wandering brothers and sisters that, at the very instant that they were conceived in their mother's womb, they took their first steps into eternity. We are to live our lives being fully conscious of this reality. The essence of a true testimony gives witness that we really do believe and live in accordance with this conception of life. That this awareness transcends the state of the material world attests to the reality of a spiritual Kingdom, and the way we handle all our daily affairs clearly shows the strength of our faith.

The Sacramental Economy

At Baptism, we become instruments through which God distributes His graces to humanity. It is our responsibility to stay faithful to God so that He can use us to carry out the mission for which we were created. We have already been made in the image and likeness of God but the supernatural anointing we receive at Baptism makes us *Children of the Light*, able to blind the forces of darkness. Clothed in the graces given to us through the sacraments, we are able to do great works for the salvation of souls. We are heirs to the Kingdom of God. If there is one thing humanity must clearly understand, it is this: the God who created each one of us is a good God, a merciful God who loves and forgives, a God whose greatest desire is the salvation of all human beings, without exception.

The Sacraments: Knowing The Weapons

Christian initiation is effected through the sacraments that lay the foundation of Christian life: the faithful are born anew by Baptism, strengthened by Confirmation and nourished by the Eucharist.

This is what the *Catechism of the Catholic* Church tells us about the sacraments of initiation:

The sacraments of Christian initiation - Baptism, Confirmation, and the Eucharist - lay the foundations of every Christian life. "The sharing in the divine nature given to men through the grace of Christ bears a certain likeness to the origin, development, and nourishing of natural life. The faithful are born anew by Baptism, strengthened by the sacrament of Confirmation, and receive in the Eucharist the food of eternal life. By means of these sacraments of Christian initiation, they thus receive in increasing measure the treasures of the divine life and advance toward the perfection of charity."

(Catechism 1212)

What is the first sacrament of Christian initiation?

The first sacrament of initiation is called Baptism because of the central rite with which it is celebrated. To baptize means to dip, or immerse, in water. One who receives Baptism is immersed in Christ's death and is raised with him "as a new creature" (2 Cor. 5:17). It is also called "bath of regeneration and renewal in the Holy Spirit" (Titus. 3:5) and "illumination" because the baptized person becomes a "child of light" (Eph. 5:8). (See Catechism 1214-1216). So, to be baptized is to be chosen. What a deep mystery and what a huge responsibility this is! Thousands of God's people went through the desert under the guidance of the great prophet Moses, without ever understanding or accepting exactly what it meant to be chosen. They frequently looked to return to the old pagan customs with which they had been contaminated during their exile in Egypt. Because of this, many died, falling into the devil's traps.

Those who did succeed in entering the *Promised Land* left their example of fidelity for all future generations, and in so doing became living stones in the economy of salvation.

Despite having passed through the desert to reach the *Promised Land* and despite receiving the Incarnated Messiah, the people of God today, once again, lack faith. Consequently, they are unable to make use of the powerful, supernatural unction they have received in Baptism. If so many of the first group of *the Chosen* failed to reach the *Promised Land*, what might we expect of the second group? We are that second group, those who have been grafted onto the original tree of *God's Chosen People.* We are called to embrace the fullness of the gift of redemption in Christ so that we may enter the Temple of the Most Holy, the *Promised Land* in Heaven.

In the *Holy Sacrifice* of the Eucharist, Jesus acts as our *Mediator* protecting us from the annihilation which would otherwise befall us as a consequence of our sins. But, if we do not cease from offending God in this earthly life, we will face a most painful purification when we die. Our responsibility is much greater than the rest of humanity because so much has been given to us.

To better understand the greatness of what it means to be a baptized Christian, we must penetrate the mystery of each one of the powerful sacraments that govern and guide our supernatural life on earth.

I offer some limited insights here into the infinite and mystical dimension of the sacraments, in the hope of inspiring the faithful to navigate more profoundly in God's Spirit so that they might gain a deeper appreciation of the immensity of the abundance of graces we have received through His Son, Jesus Christ.

The more we plumb the fathomless depths of God, the more we will understand the supernatural life. Such awareness helps us to make better use of the sacraments and to become those effective instruments of God, possessing, as Saint Paul describes it, *"treasure in earthen vessels, that the surpassing power may be of God and not from us"* (2 Cor. 4:7-8).

A Eucharistic Christian, faithful to God, is able to do wonderful things for God's Kingdom and the salvation of souls. We must wake from our slumber and decide for action. Legions of demons conspire ceaselessly against the Kingdom of God and the baptized have been sent to its defense. Everywhere, we see pagan philosophies, secular ideologies, diabolical cults and sects seducing the people of God, leading them into confusion, robbing them of spiritual strength and, ultimately, depriving them of the graces they received through the sacraments.

Baptism

Baptism is a supernatural anointing that exorcizes us from *Original Sin*. This sacrament frees us from all ancestral curses and makes us new creatures in the Spirit of God, flooding our whole being with light and filling us with God's love. It equips us with a mighty breastplate which protects us from an enemy who will relentlessly besiege our soul until the day we die.

Baptism alone is a challenge to the *Forces of Evil*. The potential in one who has been baptized is so great, that the *Enemy* wants to eliminate him, and the threat he poses, from the very moment of his conception. The Devil will do his utmost to prevent the baptized person from becoming active in the Faith and becoming a source of light that will blind those who live in darkness.

Due to our secular, materialistic culture, many Catholics have lost the experience of God in the *sacraments*. They are not aware of who they are, the enormity of the gift God has given them or of the great responsibility he has entrusted to them. The Holy Spirit's action in the baptized soul fills it with Divine Wisdom enabling him to carry out the precise mission for which he has been created. For this reason, when he dies and stands before the Divine Tribunal of Our Lord Jesus Christ, he will have no excuse.

The gift of Baptism is an eternal grace. It makes us active members of the Kingdom of God in the midst of humanity. Our participation in the *Economy of Salvation* does not end at the moment of death. United to the angels and saints with the Virgin Mary and all the Heavenly Court, we will continue fighting for souls until Jesus returns and puts an end to death, once and for all.

Yes, we have the entire Heavenly Court on our side, and the devil knows it. As Scripture tells us, many are called but, in the end, few will be chosen. Many Catholics - despite being chosen by God - abandon their commitment to Him. As a result, they fall away from the Kingdom of Light and easily succumb to the lure of the world.

Once a Catholic becomes fully aware of the magnitude of the gift of Baptism, he is permanently anointed in love, compassion, mercy and the power of God. He is inspired to live according to Christ's Gospel; true joy and gladness flood his soul and heart. He becomes a disciple, another *fisher of men*, continuing on the apostolic way the Lord has traced out for us. By walking this path, hundreds of souls will be rescued by his fidelity, sacrifice, courage and humility.

In the case of adult Baptism, it is very important that the individual catechumenate should consider the nature of the battle, and his particular circumstances, before he makes such a huge commitment. Frequently in today's culture, Catholic parents have their children baptized even though they themselves do not profess their faith. In many cases, although the parents have been estranged from the Church for many years, deep in their hearts they feel called to take their children to the Baptismal font. What great love God has for His children! No one can escape His great mercy. It is like a deep, precious secret we bear in our hearts as we travel through our earthly exile - even if we have not been faithful to the sacrament. When God anoints us with this grace, we are marked by the Seal of His Divinity and so enjoy the unconditional protection of His angels, who will always accompany us - even when we disobey God. Baptism is a clear sign that we have been chosen by God.

Christianity presents two different groups of baptized individuals. The first is those who are baptized as Catholics according to the sacrament instituted by the Lord, personally, more than two thousand years ago. The second group are Protestants baptized in the baptism of sects. Although these only began with the Reformation 500 years ago, Jesus did tell us about them during His public life, when the apostles approached him saying:

> Teacher, we saw a man casting out demons in your name, and we forbade him, because he was not following us. Jesus answered them: "Do not forbid him; for no one who does a mighty work in my name will be able soon after to speak evil of me, for he who is not against us is for us." (Mark. 9:38)

Jesus did not reject them, but it was clear that he had not called them directly. They preferred to be distant and so acted independently of Jesus, despite his being close to them. However, they did, as we are told, exorcize in his name. Jesus revealed this to us as something that would happen in Christianity; it is a mystery that only God will clarify at the end. All Christians of today who are not in union with the Catholic Church - the Church of the Apostles and of the Mother of Jesus - belong to this latter group.

God calls some laborers in the morning, others at midday and others in the afternoon, but all are paid the same wage (Matt. 20:12). This makes it clear that God has a plan for each one of us. In His mysterious providence, God's salvific action always comes through human agency: apostles; prophets; priests; preachers or simple lay faithful. In all vocations, the Lord calls at different times of life. Abraham and Moses are good examples. Abraham, the Father of Faith had lived a long pagan life before the Lord called him. Moses, too, grew up in a pagan culture with the Egyptian Pharaoh's family and was 57 years old when the Lord called him to become one of the greatest prophets in all of Sacred History.

Thousands of individuals have been called by God in the course of the centuries in ways that are totally unpredictable and incomprehensible to human reason. Each call, like each life, is unique, but in another sense, they are all part of the same universal call which is the call to do *God's Holy Will*. This is the most important call: to accept it, to obey it, to honor it and to live it by keeping God's *Commandments* and carrying our cross day by day.

The *sacraments* are the close encounters with God to which the Church calls us. They draw the faithful into deeper reflection on the mysteries of the Faith and invite each Catholic to discover the spiritual strength and gifts that he has been given so he can clearly understand the particular way he has been called to service. We must remain alert and ready to respond to that persistent prompting of the Spirit who will send us out, just as He sent Paul and Barnabas who, through prayer and fasting, were given the grace to understand and obey God's particular plan for them (Acts. 13:1-3).

Penance and Reconciliation: Confession

O nce we are baptized, we begin a preparation that can last seven to nine years before we are ready to receive Jesus in the form of the Eucharistic bread. First Holy Communion is a magnificent gift. We must prepare our heart and soul for it, becoming aware, for the first time, of the existence of sin in our life. This leads us to make what the Church calls the *Act of Contrition*. This is necessary for true reconciliation with God and prepares the baptized to become vessels of the Holy Spirit, able to hold the treasure of the Eucharist, living tabernacles of the Lord.

The sacrament of Confession - also known as the sacrament of Penance and the sacrament of Reconciliation - has been dangerously ignored by today's modernist clergy, to the point where we even see general absolution being dispensed wholesale. Entire congregations at Sunday Mass are invited to receive Holy Communion, with no consideration given to the state of their souls or whether those in serious mortal sin have any intention of renouncing their sinful lives and returning to God's friendship.

Sadly, we know that these poor priests, who have lost their way, will be burdened before the Tribunal of Jesus with the sins of all the congregations they absolved, when they violated the dignity and the precepts of this holy sacrament. Regardless of the thoughts and practice of priests regarding the sacrament of Penance, the fact is that without the preparation of a thorough Confession, the soul is unable to receive the Eucharistic grace necessary for God to do His magnificent work of reparation for the salvation of souls.

If we are not conscious of the power of the Eucharist, how can we understand the importance of confessing our sins to a priest, or the necessity of kneeling in humility to bend the spirit of pride which we allowed to enter our souls when we sinned.

It is not for nothing that Saint Paul warns us:

> Let each one, then, examine himself before eating of the bread and drinking from the cup. Otherwise, he eats and drinks his own condemnation, in not recognizing the Body. (1 Cor. 11:28-29)

What does the Apostle mean by being "prepared"? Is he not speaking of reconciliation, of contrition? He is referring directly to the efforts each of us must make if we are to be at peace with the Bread of Life, before we can dare to consume this bread as our spiritual nourishment? He is, in fact, exhorting us to examine ourselves, to confess and detach from all sin.

To be conscious of the nature of sin requires clear knowledge and understanding of what the sacrament of Reconciliation really means. To really repent, we need to know exactly what repentance means, which requires an understanding of what sin is. In Latin, the word for sin is *peccatum*, the voluntary transgression of a precept held as good. In Hebrew, the common word for sin is *Jatta'th*, which means to err.

If we accept that the Book of Genesis is not a fable or some human story, made up to get us to fear God, then we also have to accept the fact that we have been cast out of Paradise and that it was God Himself who cast us out because we sinned against Him. We sinned by succumbing to the temptation of the old serpent, Satan and compromising ourselves in relation to the spirit of disobedience. Sin is Satan. We fell by our own free will, and by our own free will we must be reconciled with God. That is why God instituted the sacrament of Reconciliation, through the risen Jesus Christ, so that, in freedom, we would willingly approach the *Tribunal of His Mercy*.

In simple terms, to deny the existence of our first parents, Adam and Eve, is to deny the existence of *Original Sin*, the *Fall*, and man's mortality. We also deny Christ because we deny the Cross, the Redemption and *the Redeemer* himself.

What does the Catechism of the Catholic Church teach us about sin?

According to the Catechism:

> Sin is an offence against reason, truth, and right conscience; it is a failure in genuine love for God and for neighbor caused by a perverse attachment to certain goods. It wounds the nature of man and injures human solidarity. It has been defined as "an utterance, a deed, or a desire contrary to the eternal law".
>
> (Catechism 1849)

A Catholic must constantly renew and maintain his soul in a state of cleanliness. Otherwise, evil will enter and sow its seeds in his heart and ruinous changes in his interior life will result. Spiritually speaking, it is very demanding to be *Eucharistic*. The enemy will do everything he can to capture a faithful soul, because such a soul creates many difficulties for his evil machinations. This sacrament is crucial if we are to remain strong in the battle against the *Powers of Darkness*.

Satan seeks to weaken the Catholic and dissuade him from Confession because he knows this sacrament gives him an opportunity to keep his prideful ego in check. It is an extraordinary gift through which we are able to make ourselves little again, by accepting the reality that we are sinners and that we depend completely on God's grace if we are to be good. Only in this way can we succeed in being the effective instruments of the Eucharist that we are supposed to be.

What does the Catechism say about this sacrament?

The Catechism tells us:

> It is called the *sacrament of conversion* because it makes sacramentally present Jesus' call to conversion, the first step in returning to the Father from whom one has strayed by sin.

> It is called the *sacrament of Penance*, since it consecrates the Christian sinner's personal and ecclesial steps of conversion, penance, and satisfaction.

> It is called the *sacrament of confession*, since the disclosure or confession of sins to a priest is an essential element of this sacrament. In a profound sense it is also a "confes-

sion" - acknowledgment and praise - of the holiness of God and of his mercy toward sinful man.

It is called the *sacrament of forgiveness,* since by the priest's sacramental absolution God grants the penitent "pardon and peace".

It is called the *sacrament of Reconciliation,* because it imparts to the sinner the love of God who reconciles: "Be reconciled to God." He who lives by God's merciful love is ready to respond to the Lord's call: "Go; first be reconciled to your brother".

(Catechism 1423-1424)

Why is the sacrament of Confession necessary after Baptism?

The new life of grace received at Baptism does not abolish the weakness of human nature or the inclination to sin (concupiscence). Christ instituted this sacrament for the conversion of the baptized person who has been separated from him by sin. (See Catechism 1425-1426)

When was this sacrament instituted?

Sacred Scripture tells us:

> On the evening of that day, the first day of the week, Jesus showed himself to his apostles. He breathed on them, and said to them: 'Receive the Holy Spirit. If you

forgive the sins of any, they are forgiven; if you retain the sins of any, they are retained'. (Jn. 20:19, 22-23)

Sin begets vice. This explains the process of spiritual corruption. Satan's main objective is to keep a person chained in mortal sin. By keeping a soul captive in his territory, the devil is able to use him against God and the Church. He uses him to infiltrate the lines of the faithful, turning him into a Judas. The conversion of a believer into a slave of the devil is done with the specific intention of keeping him inside God's lines as an enemy of God. This is how the devil carries out his most devastating attacks. It is like pitting a mother against her children and the children against their parents. The *Kingdom of Evil* divides; its power lies precisely in its ability to create division.

If we fall into mortal sin, our whole existence becomes a realm of self-loathing and despair. Joy disappears, we no longer have peace in our heart and, without really realizing it, we become instruments that disrupt and disturb our neighbor's peace. In this way we spread the contagion of our sin, contaminating other souls.

The Eucharist: Holy Communion

The Eucharist is a Catholic's greatest treasure. It is communion with the very Body and Blood of Our Lord Jesus Christ. Nothing can compare to the greatness and the wonder of this unfathomable mystery, that the God who has created everything, Who is omnipotent and all-knowing, should become a small, fragile piece of plain bread, for our sake.

God sacrifices Himself on the altar and, through the great mystery of transubstantiation, becomes this little Host, our spiritual food. This is something so incomprehensible, so absolutely transcendental that it is completely beyond human senses or intellect to fathom. It simply goes beyond us.

A Catholic, who really believes that Jesus is alive in the Eucharist, is an anointed being. He possesses an indescribable grace, a pearl beyond price. To be conscious of this mystery is to share in it. This participation makes of the mystery itself, spiritual food for all the souls with whom the believer comes in contact. He is animated by a lively faith, devoid of doubts, he sees God perfectly clearly in the Host.

When we make our First Holy Communion, we are supernaturally clothed in the mantle of everlasting life. Eating the Body of the Lord and drinking His Blood is an unsurpassable gift. It is the soul's ultimate fulfillment in this life. The demons' power is weakened in the presence of such a person and, despite wanting to destroy him, they fear being defeated by the power of Christ that he bears within him. Because of the threat that such a 'Eucharistic soldier' poses, Satan will continue fighting him until the end of his days, in an attempt to destroy his relationship with the source of his strength, namely the Eucharist.

The entire universe revolves around the Eucharist. It is thanks to the Eucharist that Christianity has survived for more than two thousand years. The people of God, who were brought out of exile in Egypt, were nourished with manna that fell from heaven. This was a foreshadowing of the Bread that would come down from Heaven, the Messiah. The Eucharist is the Bread which will sustain the new people of God throughout their pilgrimage on earth. We are nourished by the Body and Blood of Christ, who gives us the strength to remain firm and faithful in the face of the snares and terrible temptations we must endure, so we can keep going until we finally reach the door of the Kingdom of God.

The Catholic Church has suffered many attacks against the Eucharist since Vatican Council II. It is so sad to see the tremendous irreverence to the Eucharist that we witness in so many parishes, seminaries, convents and monasteries around the world. The deplorable treatment that Jesus suffers in the Eucharist today - virtually the world over - seems to be getting worse and worse as time goes on. Every day, it seems that there is a greater loss of reverence and respect for the Eucharist.

During the almost eight years of Benedict XVI's pontificate, we witnessed the quite extraordinary witness of a humble and simple man of God, who, without any great pretensions or great speeches, gave us a clear example every day, in every Eucharist that he celebrated, of how we ought to properly receive the Divine Host: on the tongue, and on our knees. This was the only way he would give Holy Communion to those who wished to receive it from him. But our Spiritual blindness is so great today, that the majority of Catholics ignore this clear and powerful message. In my travels throughout the Catholic world, I did not see any change in this practice or heard any mention of the Pope's clear recommendation. I find myself wondering: Have we become Protestants? Who are we really obeying? A Catholic parish or community, which is not focused on total adoration of the Most Blessed Sacrament has, to some extent, become Protestant, and is dangerously undernourished spiritually.

Many Catholic parishes begin by losing all connection with the sacrament of Confession. As sure as night follows day, this inevitably leads to a loss of respect and reverence for the Holy Eucharist. We need to take great care not to become lukewarm or complacent in our attitude or comportment with regard to the Holy Eucharist. It is essential that we stay focused on what, or rather Who, the Eucharist really is. As Saint Ignatius of Antioch reminds us, "In the Eucharist, we break the bread that offers the medicine of immortality; the antidote to death and the food that makes us live forever in Christ Jesus".

What does the Catechism say about the Eucharist?

The Catechism tells us:

> The Eucharist is the real sacrifice of the Body and Blood of Our Lord Jesus Christ. He "instituted the Eucharis-

tic sacrifice of his Body and Blood. This he did in order to perpetuate the sacrifice of the cross throughout the ages until he should come again, and so to entrust to his beloved spouse, the Church, a memorial of his death and resurrection; a sacrament of love, a sign of unity, a bond of charity, a Paschal banquet 'in which Christ is consumed, the mind is filled with grace, and a pledge of future glory is given to us'."

(Catechism 1323)

The Eucharist fills us with every grace and heavenly blessing, it fortifies our pilgrimage in this life, it makes us desire eternal life and unites us to the whole heavenly Court.

When did Jesus institute the Eucharist?

Sacred Scripture tells us:

> At the Last Supper, on the night he was betrayed, our Saviour instituted the Eucharistic sacrifice. (1 Cor. 11:23)

Hence, the Eucharist is not a symbol. It is God himself in the person of Jesus Christ. As a child, Saint Ignatius of Antioch encountered Jesus in person. As soon as he met him, he knew He was God. While serving as one of the first bishops of the Church in Antioch, he was taken by Nero to Rome and thrown to the lions in the Roman Colosseum. His statement on the Eucharist was powerful. All Christians called for his release in Rome, but he begged them not to do so. He told them: I must be ground by the teeth of the beasts to make myself bread of life for the Church. Indeed, when he arrived at the Colosseum and was thrown to the lions, he ran to them singing psalms. That day hundreds of Romans converted to Christianity.

Where is the Ark of the Covenant?

The Ark of the Covenant is no longer an ancient repository housing the *Tablets of God's Law,* the *Sign of Manna* and Aaron's staff. It has been surpassed by the Incarnation of God in the second person of the Most Holy Trinity, Jesus Christ. That same Eucharist, Jesus, dwells with us today in the Tabernacle. As Catholics, we are the new tribe of Levi, the priesthood that God has made guardians of the Holy of Holies, present and alive in the Eucharist. We are the continuation of Judaism and we have recognized him as the Messiah since the moment of his Holy Incarnation.

We are the Gentiles who have been grafted onto the original tree of the Chosen People of Israel. God chooses from among us the sacramental priests whom he anoints for the purpose of carrying out the mystery of transubstantiation on the altar. To these priests, his ordained ministers, he gave the power to forgive or retain sins.

Jesus came to die, but once only. The mystery of transubstantiation is Christ's sacrifice on the altar; it is a 're-presentation' of his Holy Passion, Death and Resurrection. Does he die over and over? No, he dies in us, and makes himself one with us by uniting himself to our material existence, to our flesh, turning us into co-participants of his Passion, Death and Resurrection. We become, through him, mystical vessels of reparation for the salvation of the world.

We read in the *Acts of the Apostles* that, after the coming of the Holy Spirit on the Apostolic college, the apostles walked daily through the streets of Jerusalem on their way to the Temple to preach the Gospel, but not before breaking the bread in community and drinking the wine as Jesus taught them at the Last Supper, which was the First Eucharist. As they passed by, their shadow cured the sick and delivered the possessed from unclean spirits. They did not even need to place their hands on them (Acts. 5:15). Why? Because of the power of the Body and Blood of the Lord that they had just consumed in community. They were bearers of the Living God. We see, then, that, from its first beginnings, the Church was built on the spiritual foundations of the Eucharist. It is a vital and absolute power, that makes us strong enough to confront the forces that threaten us and try to keep us from carrying out the work which the Lord has entrusted us with in this life: the salvation of souls.

Confirmation

The sacrament of Confirmation possesses many elements that can be said to be mystical in nature. It is a powerful spiritual weapon that, when lived fully consciously, can render incalculable service to the Church's mission to save souls. Even though this sacrament is conferred at quite a young age - usually fifteen - the spiritual anointing received goes beyond one's physical years. Because it is of supernatural origin, the sacrament of Confirmation is outside of time and space, existing in the *Eternal Present* of God.

With a deep understanding of this anointing, we are more able to appreciate the wonderful gift of Pentecost. While Baptism is a powerful exorcism and anointing of the Holy Spirit, the sacrament of Confirmation is the conscious encounter with the baptized individual's apostolic mission. It activates the divine power deposited in us at Baptism, illumining our entire being and strengthening us in the love of God - a power that can only be likened to the fire of Pentecost.

Our Catholic faith does not usually manifest this fire of the Holy Spirit externally, in an emotional way, as we see with evangelical sects. Through the mystical power of the Eucharist, our whole being can assimilate this power of God in the profound silence of His love, fortifying us to carry out the mission in His Church for which we were created.

The imposition of the bishop's hands at Confirmation does not happen in an extraordinary event. No one rests necessarily in the Spirit. There are no convulsions or emotional reactions, because a Catholic already has the wonderful gift of the Eucharistic unction. That is why the effusion of the Holy Spirit, with the imposition of the bishop's hands, is recreated in the depth of one's being, as a current of living water that runs serenely through the soul just as streams flowing in the Heavenly Jerusalem, amid the peace and joy of the presence of God. The soul is lifted to the height of God the Father, received in His arms and filled with His love. Then he is sent out to continue his desert pilgrimage in the quest for souls for the Kingdom.

A person's whole being is transformed by this sacrament. A new psychology of life is acquired. Spiritual instincts and senses are awakened which were inactive before. The soul's inner vision opens up and the spiritual world is perceived as a present and permanent reality. Acute and exact discernment emerges, detecting the action of evil with much wisdom, within the security of the love of God. Impulses are awakened, prompting 'the confirmed' to act according to the Spirit of God.

Some Catholics reading this description of the effects of Confirmation may feel it does not accord with their own personal experience of the sacrament. This is something that can be positive. It may well be the beginning of a new evangelization, an opportunity to appropriate a deeper awareness of mysteries of one's own faith and to decide to become more active in our appointed mission. The apostles were sent out for the first time, before they received the Holy Spirit. Jesus gave them the power to do things they could not have imagined possible.

When they returned and met Jesus, they were astounded by the wonders they had carried out in His name. Even Judas Iscariot was given the same power to cure and deliver souls despite his future treachery. This was all an anticipation of what was to come. Such is the mystery of God's unconditional fidelity.

Confirmation gives us the spiritual wings that allow us to reach great heights in the universe of Divine Love. We can see the people of God gathered in Antioch, praying and praising God:

> While they were worshiping the Lord and fasting, the Holy Spirit said, "Set apart for me Barnabas and Saul for the work to which I have called them." Then, completing their fasting and prayer, they laid hands on them and sent them off. (Acts. 13:1-3)

We see from the apostles' first missions how they are clothed in a strength that was not natural. They show no signs of doubt or fear. They are supported by great wisdom and perfectly guided regarding where, when and how they must go and what they are to say and do.

Jesus promised that he would be with us all the days of our life (Matt. 28:20). It is so encouraging to observe how faithful He has been to this promise through the centuries of Christianity.

From beginning to end, the message of salvation declares open war on sin, and Satan is sin. We are not foretelling something that is to happen in the future. We are proclaiming the power of a kingdom that is among us now. We are not preparing to fight some future encounter; we are already in the heat of battle and the enemy rages all around us, as the Book of Revelation reminds:

> Rejoice then, O heaven and you that dwell therein! But woe to you, O earth and sea, for the devil has come down to you in great wrath, because he knows that his time is short. (Rev. 12:12)

Our understanding of reality must be steeped in an awareness of this spiritual battle. The essence of every sacrament, flowing from the source of all life and power, emanates from the Sacred Heart of Jesus, present and alive, in the Sacrament of sacraments, the Holy Eucharist. To be armed with this sacrament, we must prepare meticulously and undergo a genuine and sincere conversion. Once a bishop's hands are placed on the head of an individual being confirmed, the immense spiritual capital of many generations of martyrs flows through the heart and soul of the one being anointed. It is a shower of the most sacred of oils, which descends directly from heaven to defend souls from eternal perdition. Its power flows forth and becomes active in the depth of the soul. It is the true fire that comes from on High that takes the supernatural action already received at Baptism and First Holy Communion, and transforms it into the fire of the love of God that covers the whole earth.

How many Catholics really know what happens spiritually when they receive this sacrament? Perhaps a great percentage have died without being consciously part of the active militia in the battle for which they were born. Perhaps one of the saddest encounters with Christ that a person can have is to discover, at the end of his life, that the gifts he received were wasted. Many souls do not attain eternal salvation because of the infidelity of a baptized Catholic. Those of us who have been called and confirmed must take in the mystery of this sacrament. Let us not go on as soldiers who set up camp on the premises of the enemy, eating the fruits of the garden of exile. Let us resist the poisonous pride and illusion of this passing world. We have been confirmed to defend the Church, to save souls every day and everywhere. Each step we take has been entrusted to us spiritually for Her defense, Her custody and protection, where our example, our testimony of life, our loyalty and obedience to God are an inspiration for all.

If we wish to reflect on the way that a purgatory is built in life, we must examine our actions in the world and how committed we are to the spiritual tasks God has entrusted to us. We recall how much time we have wasted in our lives, chasing the wind, seeking after earthly goals and pleasures, ignoring the transcendental aspect of our acts in relation to eternal life. God wills us to be saints – perfect as He is holy and perfect (1 Pet. 1:15). Anyone who looks for another way is removing himself from the center of this truth. The sacrament of Confirmation is an ocean of unexploited power and wisdom that is, to a large degree, ignored by most Catholics.

Let me say that in this sacrament we have been given the power of the Holy Spirit to be able to carry out the mission for which God created us. As Jesus told us, we will be able to do the things that he did, and even greater.

Some Catholics will not identify with my presentation, and this is understandable. God has given us all free will, and we will not always agree on everything, but we can all agree that we who belong to Christ must live strictly according to the Gospel that He Himself taught us. There is no other way. The only other alternative would be to disobey him, that is, to live in sin.

It might also seem to many who live a Catholic faith conveniently adapted to their philosophies of natural life, that I am presenting a God who is strict and vengeful. The Lord is just. It is one thing to present oneself before the *Tribunal of the Lord* at the end of this life with a heart given completely to Him and quite another to appear before him having lived a life strictly according to one's human will, a life that has been far from God despite having received the anointing of the sacraments and the fullness of revealed truth.

From my own personal experience with God I would plead with every believer to take great care to ensure they are well prepared before they stand before the Tribunal of the Lord. From the one who receives much, much is expected.

What does the Catechism say about this sacrament?

The Catechism tells us:

> In the Old Testament the prophets announced that the Spirit of the Lord would rest on the awaited Messiah for his saving mission. However, this fullness of the Spirit was not to remain uniquely the Messiah's, but was to be communicated to the whole messianic people. Having been conceived by the Holy Spirit, his whole life and mission were carried out in total communion with the Holy Spirit, whom the Father gave him "without measure"

Filled with the Holy Spirit the apostles began to proclaim "the mighty works of God". By the laying on of hands, they imparted to the newly baptized the gift of the Holy Spirit. Since then the Church has continued, throughout the centuries, to live by the Spirit and to impart him to Her children. (See Catechism 1286-1288)

Why is this Sacrament called Confirmation or Chrismation?

This anointing highlights the name "Christian," which means "anointed" and derives from that of Christ himself whom God "anointed with the Holy Spirit." This rite of anointing has continued ever since, in both East and West. For this reason, the Eastern Churches call this sacrament Chrismation, anointing with chrism, or myron which means "chrism." In the West, Confirmation suggests both the ratification of Baptism, thus completing Christian initiation, and the strengthening of baptismal grace.

(Catechism 1289)

What is the effect of Confirmation?

The effect of Confirmation is the full effusion of the Holy Spirit, as it was conferred on the apostles on the day of Pentecost: "From this fact, Confirmation brings an increase and deepening of Baptismal grace. [Confirmation ...] roots us more deeply in divine filiation which makes us cry out: "Abba, Father" (Rom. 8:15)

Furthermore, the Catechism instructs us that Confirmation:

- Unites us more firmly to Christ;
- Increases the gifts of the Holy Spirit in us;
- Renders our bond with the Church more perfect;
- Gives us a special strength of the Holy Spirit to spread and defend the faith by word and action as true witnesses of Christ, to confess the name of Christ boldly, and never to be ashamed of the Cross. (See Catechism 1303)

Who can Receive this Sacrament?

"Every baptized person not yet confirmed can and should receive the sacrament of Confirmation" (Catechism 1306) ... and, "To receive Confirmation one must be in a state of grace".

(Catechism 1310)

I would like to add something very important here. It is very common to hear in charismatic groups about "baptism in the spirit". I have observed that many Catholics who lack good doctrinal formation, are under the impression that they have not received this baptism before, and believe that Catholics who have not received "baptism in the spirit" are somehow lacking the anointing needed to be able to live their faith in fullness. It is worth clarifying that, when the Church administers the sacrament of Baptism to a soul, he is placed on a supernatural plane. And, when this person approaches the sacrament of the Eucharist, he is submerged in a spiritual dimension of extraordinary and incomprehensible mystical transcendence that is beyond human reason; his whole being is flooded with this sanctifying grace of the Body and Blood of Our Lord Jesus Christ, the Bread of Life.

Keeping these very important factors in mind, we can add that, when the bishop imposes his hands to confer the sacrament of Confirmation, extraordinary things do not happen at the external level; everything happens in perfect tranquility. Why is it that this very important, transcendent sacrament is imparted amid much serenity, when in a charismatic event the imposition of hands, even by a layman at the end of a seminar of Life in the Spirit, is accompanied by extraordinary manifestations, 'resting in the spirit' and in some cases the gift of tongues and prophecy?

The answer does not lie in comparing the two events, but in a proper conception of what each one comprises. One who receives the sacrament of Confirmation is duly prepared, confessed and catechized for this sacrament and his spirit, recipient of this grace, is profoundly penetrated by the Eucharistic gift that he already possesses. Through this, such an immense blessing is assimilated that it elevates the being to a transcendent spiritual level. This gift is received entirely mystically, in the depth of the soul. This is not necessarily accompanied by emotional or external manifestations of any sort.

The remarkable manifestations we sometimes see occur at the end of a Life in the Spirit seminar, for example, are the result of a progressive edification through a series of catechesis regarding the action of the Holy Spirit in the life of the baptized individual. This progression of preparatory events gives the person a spiritual, psychological and emotional predisposition that, at the moment of approaching what is known as *baptism in the spirit*, his whole anticipation erupts in emotions that manifest in the action of the spirit through *resting in the spirit* – which is the total relaxation of the instincts and senses which overpowers the individual physically. This experience requires an encounter of such magnitude that it opens the baptized person to the natural flow that the Holy Spirit must have in his life. Then some *charismatic gifts*, such as speaking in tongues, which were received much earlier sacramentally, and have lain dormant, may awaken.

The important thing here is the need to use correct theological language so as not to confuse weak Catholics or those ignorant of their faith. We should not speak of a "baptism in the spirit" without first making clear to people that they have already received the Holy Spirit when they were baptized, usually as infants. A better term to use is "renewal in the spirit". This safeguards against the danger of falling into Protestant practices which lack a solid eucharistic foundation. Such individuals easily fall prey to a superficial emotionalism because, without the power of the Eucharist, the Christian lacks the strength necessary to fortify him to assimilate the action of the Holy Spirit in a mystical way.

The term "baptism in the spirit" has Pentecostal and Evangelical origins. It is not an error or a sin for Catholics to receive it but it is confusing if not well explained to those not properly formed in the Catholic faith.

Holy Orders

The Catechism tells us:

> "Holy Orders is the sacrament through which the mission entrusted by Christ to his apostles continues to be exercised in the Church until the end of time."
>
> (Catechism 1536)

Why is it called the Sacrament of Holy Orders?

In the Church there are established bodies which Sacred Tradition calls *Orders.*

> "The word *order* in Roman antiquity designated an established civil body, especially a government body.
>
> (Catechism 1537)

Again, from the Catechism:

> "Integration into one of these bodies in the Church was accomplished by a rite called ordination, a religious and liturgical act which was a consecration, a blessing or a sacrament. Today the word "ordination" is reserved

for the sacramental act which integrates a man into the order of bishops, presbyters, or deacons, and goes beyond a simple election, designation, delegation, or institution by the community, for it confers a gift of the Holy Spirit that permits the exercise of a "sacred power" (sacra potestas) which can come only from Christ himself through his Church. Ordination is also called consecratio, for it is a setting apart and an investiture by Christ himself for his Church. The laying on of hands by the bishop, with the consecratory prayer, constitutes the visible sign of this ordination."

(Catechism 1538)

What place does Holy Orders have in the economy of salvation?

This sacrament was prefigured in the Old Testament in the service of the Levites, in the priesthood of Aaron, and in the institution of the seventy "elders" (Num. 11:24-25). These prefigurations found their fulfillment in Christ Jesus, "the one mediator between God and men" (1 Tim. 2:5), the "high priest after the order of Melchizedek" (Heb. 5:10; 6:20). Christ's priesthood is present in the ministerial priesthood. And that is why Saint Thomas Aquinas tells us, "Christ alone is the true priest; the rest are his ministers". (Commentarium in Epistolam ad Haebreos, c. 7, lect. 4).

In the exercise of their sacred ministry, ordained priests speak and act, not on their own authority, or by mandate or delegation of the community, but in the Person of Christ who is the head, and in the name of the Church. Therefore, the ministerial priesthood differs in essence, but not in degree, from the common priesthood instituted by Christ for all the faithful. (See Catechism 1552-1553)

One of the most dramatic of my mystical encounters with God was the vision I experienced of the spiritual battle confronting the priesthood. A layperson is normally subjected to temptation by the lower forces of the demonic army made up of condemned souls, demonized human beings. A priest, on the other hand, is tempted by the fallen angels. These are well armed when they come to tempt him because the priest is the devil's greatest human adversary. He is the only one who possesses the power to absolve sins and break the fetters binding the sinner, and so freeing him from Satan's clutches. Through the *Mystery of Transubstantiation*, by turning the bread and wine into the real Body and Blood of the Lord, the priest makes present the Person of Jesus.

When appointed by a bishop, a priest has the power to exorcize the demonically possessed. He has the authority to join a couple in the sacrament of Matrimony, constituting a vital force of the life of the Church, placing them and their future children at the center of the miracle of the wedding at Cana. He bathes them all in the water that Jesus transformed into wine, which is His own Blood, through which we are sealed and chosen by God as children of His Kingdom. A priest can receive a new Christian into the Church by administering the sacrament of Baptism and unites him with the main force of salvation of the pilgrim Church, through the anointing of the sacraments. He can help the dying through the rite of Extreme Unction, giving the soul the protection of the Church as it emerges from the physical body to the spiritual realm. The presence of a faithful priest is a beacon of light amid the darkness of this world.

Through time, Christianity navigates the turbulent waters of earthly life, engaging in the great battle with the Enemy of Souls, who seeks to prevent souls from receiving the gift of eternal salvation in Jesus Christ. The Church which stands on the Blood of Jesus, gives the strength and refuge to its Pilgrim People as they pass through the valley of exile.

God prepared the Incarnation of His Son through a pedagogy lasting many centuries. He began by calling Abraham, whom He created and destined to be the Father of Faith. Soon after, we have the first presentation of the priesthood in the person of Melchizedek (Heb. 5:10). This mysterious king of Salem receives Abraham's thanksgiving offering to God for victory in battle, offering a sacrifice of bread and wine on the altar.

As mankind awaited the Messiah, God prepared them through His chosen instruments. From Abraham came Isaac, and from him, Jacob. From Jacob came the twelve patriarchs from which the twelve tribes of Israel originated. One of these was the priestly tribe of Levi, the descendants of Aaron. These were charged with offering sacrifice to God for the expiation of sin - their own and that of the people - and were entrusted with the guardianship of the Ark of the Covenant.

With the Incarnation of the Divine Word, Jesus Christ, a new priesthood is established. The Resurrected Son, seated at the right hand of His Father in Heaven, is constituted sole priest of expiation for the sins of all humanity. Through Baptism, we become priests, prophets and kings so that through this supernatural, sacramental anointing, we are able to make up what is lacking in the *Mystical Body*. This is necessary for the fulfillment of the *Economy of Salvation*, when Christ will return with His angels and put an end to death forever. This knowledge of

Sacred History, as well as God's redeeming work in our lives, allows us to better appreciate who we are, and to what we have been called.

We live in critical times now, owing to the secularization of our civilization. The worship of material things, of creation rather than Creator, has brought about a *culture of death*. Today, our Church, which the Lord has called to be holy, an image of God, has become more a reflection of society. Rather than being a beacon of light to rescue souls from the darkness, the Church has become largely conformed to the world.

It is tragic to see the poor formation priests receive today. Traditional seminaries, where students were formed in sound doctrine and prepared as apostles, ready to face the storms of the world with an unwavering faith and unconditional love for the Church, have largely disappeared. Today's seminarians are often trained in secular universities, where the professors of theology are godless men, completely without faith. The devastating effect that this has had on the pastoral life of the Church is incalculable. It is also sad to see so many traditional religious communities no longer following their mystical founders. They have fallen prey to humanist psychology and pernicious progressive theologies imbued with the spirit of the New Age. We are at a crucial juncture; these are major issues for the Church. We must take decisive action if we are to move forward.

The priesthood today is in crisis. It has been infiltrated by malevolent influences and groups of sexual deviants that have systematically corrupted great swathes of people within the Church. These traitorous individuals do not belong to the Church, in spirit, or in truth. They are opportunists, seeking to satisfy their depraved appetites, but who find in the Church a good Mother that does not reject them; that forgives them over and over, and waits untiringly for their conversion. Jesus taught us: "The sons of this world are wiser in their own generation than the sons of light" (Luke. 16:8).

These *Judas* priests must be called to a true conversion or be dismissed to leave the Church in peace. We need to be brave because we are responsible before God for our Church. We cannot stand idly by in the face of this horrific spectacle, where homosexuals and pedophiles, heretics lost in the New Age, are allowed to continue destroying the image of the Church throughout the world.

I have repeatedly seen the spirit of New Age devastate religious communities. They get caught up in the enneagram, yoga, reiki, magic and other bizarre practices. As sure as night follows day, this then leads to the total destruction of the spiritual life of the community which leads to the complete absence of vocations. Once the New Age spirit infects a religious community, its members will usually become filled with such arrogance which makes it impossible to reason with them. They fall into disobedience, openly defy legitimate Church authority and usually disobey their superiors. Sometimes convents and monasteries will declare themselves independent and seize their Order's property and funds that they have been charged with administering. Some of these are turned into lucrative New Age centers offering all sorts of dubious spiritualities, exotic cults and pseudo-religions.

In Rochester, New York, I once came across a priest who broke away from the Church and persuaded his four thousand parishioners to secede from the diocese and create a new Catholicism. Not only was he successful, he also managed to keep the parish building and all its money. He appointed two women priests and founded "the new catholic church". Today he has some eight thousand faithful and is calling on other priests to follow his example.

Despite all of this, we have the assurance of Jesus' promise, that the gates of hell would not prevail against the Church, (Matt. 16:18). This is not the first time, nor will it be the last, that the Church has been beset by such evils. She has experienced similar, even worse, periods in her history. At the time of the Inquisition, the Church was riven by dissent and rebellion, to the point where it became impossible to discern who was with God and who with the devil. Everything supernatural ended up becoming suspect and was, in almost all cases, eradicated. The confusion was so great at the time, that hundreds of genuine mystics in the Church were burnt alive or put to death in other ways.

There is no *panacea* for countering these evils. Old solutions will not be effective today because we live in different times. The *Forces of Darkness* invent new strategies to suit the times. Their ploys and dark practices may appear the same on the surface but they are fueled by satanic poison introduced from other sources and in other ways. This is why it is vital that faithful believers unite to pray and fast, to implore God for discernment to help them to combat these evils that come straight from the pit of hell.

Throughout the centuries, one of the weapons, which the devil likes to employ most frequently to destroy families and the Church, is sexual deviancy. It is always the same perversion but the devil regularly injects it with fresh poison. In our generation, Satan first succeeded in convincing the secular world, and human science, that homosexuality, lesbianism, bestiality, transsexualism and other perversions are normal states and must be accepted as such. Then he turned his attention to the Church, which he has already contaminated with vice. With relative ease, he persuaded Her to accept the world's values. This is why we see the wholesale propagation of these perversions in clerical and religious life today. This is devastating because the Catholic priesthood is a vital force for the defense of sinners. It provides our greatest strength; the Holy Eucharist.

It is important that priests make a serious and sincere effort to regularly examine their conscience. The following questions are quite personal in nature, but, if answered honestly, may well provide a useful tool for helping the priest to see clearly the reality of how he currently stands in the eyes of God and the Church. With such an understanding, real change becomes possible.

- Who am I?
- Do I know for what I was consecrated?
- Am I conscious of the reason for the anointing of my hands?
- Do I know how to use the weapons entrusted to me for the salvation of souls?
- Do I believe in the real presence of Christ in the Eucharist?
- Do I really think I have the power to forgive sins?
- Do I know that I am responsible before God for every soul who comes to me?

- Do I know that, if I am a faithful priest,
  no infernal power can endure my presence
  when I raise my consecrated hands and invoke
  Jesus' name?
- Do I know that everything my hands bless
  is transformed into spirit, that is, into a
  supernatural state?
- Do I know what it is to be an unfaithful priest
  or one disobedient to hierarchy?
- Do I know the dimension to which my soul
  gravitates if I am an active homosexual priest?
- Am I a priest who preaches heresies from the
  pulpit and teaches errors to the faithful?
- Am I sexually promiscuous?
- Am I a dishonest, covetous and ambitious priest
  of material things, hungry for human power, or an
  oppressor of the sacred and of the supernatural life
  of the faithful, despising popular devotions?

If you are a priest who is unable to answer these questions as you know a faithful priest should, I would warn you that, based on the mystical experience I have had with the Lord, if you do not repent now and change your ways, you will become the food of demons, who will torment you during your life, and even more so upon death when you confront your greatest temptation. You are in serious danger of going to hell the moment you die. No one in this earthly life has greater responsibility before the *Tribunal of God* than a priest or a consecrated religious person. No one has a greater opportunity to sanctify himself in this life than the priest or religious. On the other hand, no one is in greater danger of being condemned. Just as God gives special graces to a faithful priest to allow him to carry out the weighty task of defending souls from eternal damnation, so does Satan dispense special assistance to the unfaithful priest to help him prosper in the material world. In the end, Satan will use an unfaithful priest to wound the Church and steal hundreds of souls from God. He seeks revenge against God by causing scandals. He overpowers priests, who are consecrated vessels of the Eucharist, and exploits their sins to kill the hope and faith of weak souls.

Many priests today are not conscious of who they really are or who they are meant to be. Some are children of the light but others have become instruments of Satan and children of the darkness. These are living in great spiritual danger. As members of the Catholic Church, we are all urgently called to tackle this situation, praying to God for the conversion of these priests and praying that the seminary education will return to sound doctrine and the Sacred Tradition of the Church. If seminaries do not return to the traditional formation of the Church, we will continue to ordain worldly, people-pleasing priests who, rather than really helping the poor lost faithful, leave them lying on the road, dying from the wounds inflicted by secular materialism.

The majority of seminaries are sending out priests empty-handed into an amoral and seductive world that waits to devour them, and this is exactly what ends up happening. They are swallowed up by the world as soon as they receive their first pastoral appointment. These are priests who lack the solid foundation of a mystical formation. They have no spirituality, no love of the sacraments, no respect for obedience, no knowledge of the enemy they face, and no proper prayer life. They are completely ignorant of the need to prepare their souls through fasting, abstinence, mortification and penance. Such words are unheard of in most seminaries today. I have known seminarians to be formed without a personal relation with the Holy Eucharist or a love of the Most Blessed Sacrament. They do not have a friendship with the Blessed Virgin Mary, and so remain ignorant of the spiritual strength of the Holy Rosary. They have an aversion to popular devotions and are totally skeptical about the supernatural life which God's Revelation has made known to us. They do not believe in the existence of Purgatory or hell, nor do they believe Satan to be a real person. Consequently, they are completely unaware of the action of evil in our lives. Not surprisingly, then, they have no appreciation of the work of the Holy Spirit in their priesthood.

Some might think I am exaggerating here and will, perhaps, find it difficult to accept the enormity of what we are facing. That is understandable. But, doing nothing is not acceptable. We have a serious responsibility to defend the Church that has been entrusted to us by the Lord. What we leave behind is what future generations will inherit, and the Lord will judge us on the inheritance we leave. It is my sincere hope that these lines will be read slowly, pondered carefully and find a home in faithful hearts.

Is there hope? Thankfully, the answer is a categorical and unequivocal 'Yes'. There is a great deal of hope, in fact. His name is Jesus Christ and he makes all things new. He forgives and forgets our sins. Now is the time for us to fall on our knees before the Crucified Lord begging him to rescue us, to enlighten us, and to help us to reclaim the territories we have lost to the enemy. We must rebuild the edifice of priestly and religious life without delay.

God is always with us. He wants us to take control of what has been given to us, of what he has entrusted to us. I believe that the state of spiritual darkness, which we are about to enter, will be so dense that, with the right preparation, we may be able to capitalize greatly on the opportunity it presents to us to renew the Church and bring back to God many of those who are lost and wounded in this perverse and degenerate world.

It is time to be those *fishers of men* for the Kingdom of God. People are being oppressed by the darkness and they must be rescued. We, the Catholic Church, must do this because we have been given the full revelation of the truth and the weapons for the task. Too many souls are falling into the abyss. We must work much harder to be saints because, then, the devil will not be able to touch us and we will be able to snatch millions of souls from his grasp.

In the end, many Christians separated from Mother Church will enter into the fullness of the faith and embrace a Eucharistic life. However, many others will be consumed by secularism and the beast of materialism, which seduces even the strongest. Many sects will disappear because they will not survive this battle, clinging only to the Word of God or a biblical school. It will be very difficult to attain the Kingdom without the Eucharist. Those who do succeed will be very wounded by the beast of the world and will have to resolve many issues in Purgatory. Undaunted, let us celebrate the gift of the priesthood and pray to the Lord to give us holy and courageous priests, together with religious and laity, who are able to understand the meaning of martyrdom.

There are countless kinds of religious orders. The richness of the Church is boundless when it comes to the diversity of charisms and spiritualities which God has given His Church through the ages. Each cycle of humanity produces its own particular devotions, spiritualities and practices within the Faith. God's creative power works permanently in His Church. He guides Her and adorns Her with the most precious of jewels.

This earthly life is a school for our souls, and our task is to know God, to learn to obey God and to discover the love of God. The final result of our earthly life will be to graduate in the love of God when we appear before His *Divine Tribunal*, preceded by the person of Jesus. When someone is a consecrated priest or religious, he or she is married to Jesus. This really means that God gives that chosen individual the grace that the rest of humanity will receive only at the end of life, on entering the fullness of the spiritual world. This is something few religious and priests realize, and this ignorance is the cause of the weakening of so many vocations in the priestly and religious life today.

Like the angels, we were called to embrace the love of God in all its fullness. They were created knowing God, obeying God, and loving Him perfectly, which presents us with something of a mystery. Why did they fall from grace? Obviously, we cannot understand a supernatural event of such magnitude with a limited human intellect that cannot begin to grasp the eternal sense of being.

We find the truth revealed in the Book of Genesis relating to man's *Original Fall*. We see that Adam and Eve were created to enjoy the presence and company of God forever and not to die. Were they able to know God well, to obey and love Him before the Fall? Did they have the same capacity or pure intellect as the angels? Most likely, we will not have these answers during this life. We do know, from Sacred Scripture, that we were created inferior to the angels. But what this means, and its implications for the *Economy of Salvation*, is another question.

Knowing what happened to the angels and to Adam and Eve, helps us understand that God created angels and man to learn to live in Him, to be His, to exist only for Him, but without forcing them to do so. In other words, to be chosen during this earthly life, for what we could otherwise only hope for at the end of it. This is the greatest gift, the greatest honor and the greatest responsibility, and this is precisely what the consecration of priests and religious signifies. If we have received the fullness of an intimate relationship with God through the person of His Son, by our marriage to him, we no longer belong to the world.

By His Incarnation, Jesus gave us a priesthood. This supernatural anointing of the Spirit enables us to conceive, in the depth of our soul, the need for such a marriage, the need to discover the virtue of obedience, to be able to live it in faith and to establish our heart in the heart of the First Commandment.

In the Catholic Church, we have consecrated lay people and Third Orders; Catholics – both men and women – who commit themselves to the Church under oath to specific religious congregations, and they are accepted as a force of pastoral support. These consecrated people are a powerful cell of the Church because these individuals are much more committed than the ordinary laity, while continuing to live their family lives with all the struggles, concerns and everyday tasks which this demands. This makes them important instruments in the evangelization of people who are normally out of reach of the clergy and religious.

Third Order members are often able to rescue religious from communities in danger of self-annihilation because of New Age practices or other grave threats. In this way they may serve as essential columns of support for the Church in her many skirmishes with evil.

Holy Matrimony

God, who is love, created man and woman out of love, and called them to love. When He created them, He called them to an intimate communion of life and love in Holy Matrimony; "... they are no longer two but one" (Matt. 19:6).

Blessing them, God said to them: "Be fruitful and multiply". (Gen. 1:28)

Why did God institute marriage and how does sin threaten it?

The conjugal union of man and woman, founded and equipped with its own laws by the Creator, is by its nature ordered to the communion and good of the couple and for the begetting and education of children. In keeping with the original divine plan, this conjugal union is made indissoluble when Christ declares: "What therefore God has joined together, let no man put asunder." (Mark. 10:9)

The Catechism tell us:

> Every man experiences evil around him and within himself. This experience makes itself felt in the rela-

tionships between man and woman. Their union has always been threatened by discord, a spirit of domination, infidelity, jealousy and conflicts that can escalate into hatred and separation.

(Catechism 1606)

However, in His infinite mercy, God gives man and woman the grace to achieve the union of their lives in harmony with His original plan. (See Catechism 1608)

What does the Old Testament teach about marriage?

God helped His people, primarily through the teaching of the Law and the Prophets, to deepen their understanding of the unity and indissolubility of marriage. God's nuptial covenant with Israel prepared and prefigured the new covenant established by Jesus Christ, the Son of God, with his Bride, the Church. (See Catechism 1609-1611)

What new element did Christ give marriage?

Christ not only restored the original order of marriage, but elevated it to the dignity of a sacrament, giving the spouses the special grace to live their union as symbol of the love of Christ for his Bride, the Church. "Husbands, love your wives, as Christ loved the Church" (Eph. 5:25). (For further information see the *Catechism of The Catholic Church* 1612-1614).

Is everyone obliged to get married?

Marriage is not an obligation for everyone, principally because God has called some men and women to follow the Lord Jesus in a life of virginity or celibacy for the Kingdom of Heaven. These give up the great good of Matrimony to concern themselves primarily with the Lord's concerns and to please Him. They are a sign of the supreme love of Christ and of the ardent hope for His glorious return. Looking at what is going on in the world today in regard to marriage, it is very clear that marriage, as we know it, as Christ instituted it, as God presented and established it in the course of the sacred history of His people, is being threatened to its very foundations.

God's family is the nucleus of all goodness and the nest of His love. It bears fruit for the Church: wives and husbands, priests and religious, consecrated laymen and chaste believers, all of them as children of the family of God. It is no surprise, then, that, in these end times, the *Forces of Darkness* are focused on the destruction of the family, an institution that provides the seeds of all the vocations flowing from the human family.

So-called 'gay marriage' is the most execrable abomination that evil has ever instituted in all of human history. It is the ultimate affront to God and it emanates from the very bowels of hell. It is one of the clearest signs that the world, as we know it, is rapidly coming to an end. It is a clear indication that a sweeping change is about to come to humanity.

These observations are not intended as some sort of terrifying prophecy of chastisement. My aim here is simply to try to get the chosen children of God to wake up and become more aware of their responsibilities. When you look out the window at your neighbor's house and see a wife being unfaithful, children using drugs or involved in prostitution or crime, and a father coming home drunk and abusing his wife and children, you know that it is a only a matter of time before that family disintegrates. Well, if we look at the world today, we see that disaster is upon us. It would seem inevitable that the human family is on a path of self-destruction.

There is so much darkness. The sin and dysfunction I describe above might not be evident in every neighborhood, but the decadence in our society is like a poisonous gas rising from the abyss contaminating everyone and everything with which it comes into contact, including the Church. It is choking us. We feel it everywhere. True Christian parents are having the most difficult time to keep their children from falling into the putrid waters of today's culture. It is not easy for them to find other families and individuals with a solid faith, who live in accordance with the values and precepts of the Catholic religion and the Sacred Tradition that has come down to us from our ancestors.

Mankind is so lost today, and the culture so far gone, that I am sure my words will sound to many like the fundamentalist rantings of a right-wing fanatic. I can only assure you that humanity urgently needs to turn back from the brink before it is too late. We must start to live once more *the* basic teachings of Christ, if we are to have any hope of survival. As a matter of urgency, we need to rescue the sacrament of Matrimony because marriage is God's plan for mankind; it is the basic way of living our Faith and observing God's Commandments. You might ask, 'What can I do to help rescue a humanity that has gone so far astray from God?' Perhaps you feel confounded by today's fast-paced world or you feel overwhelmed by the world's complete acceptance of the sin that has become so fashionable and an integral part of society today. We must begin by striving for personal holiness, by looking to radically change ourselves. We need to examine our hearts to see just how prepared we are to respond to the state of the world around us and to witness to the Faith, in our places of work, in our families and parish communities.

No matter what is happening in our life at present, we need to wake up and take decisive action. We need to make our voices heard. We need to express our anguish and concerns to those who are far from God. We must go out into the world, to the areas in which we find ourselves - those God has entrusted to us - and begin to speak to people about God and eternal life. We must teach them that life continues when we die and that we are only at the beginning of an eternal journey, one that is without end. We must let them know that all that we do in our short earthly lives here is going to decide how we spend the rest of eternity.

We must share, with all the souls we meet, the knowledge we have of the responsibilities that have been given to us as human beings. While we still have time, we have to let the people know our potential to advance towards a future in God, by waking up spiritually. When we defend our territory as a family of God, we join in a real battle against the forces of evil who seek our ruin. Saint Paul tells us:

For our struggle is not with flesh and blood but with the principalities, with the powers, with the world rulers of this present darkness, with the evil spirits in the heavens. (Eph. 6:12)

We have been given God's own power to defend our spiritual territories. How we are received is not important. What matters is that what we proclaim about the Kingdom of God will never be lost. God's Word tells us:

So shall my word be that goes forth from my mouth; It shall not return to me empty, but shall do what pleases me, achieving the end for which I sent it. (Isa. 55:11)

God will make use of our efforts in some way, somehow. The economy of *Evangelization*, of spreading the Gospel Truth, is always rich and rewarding, even when we do not see its fruits in this life. We must be fearless witnesses of God, always and everywhere, for as long as we live. Who else is going to pass on the Faith to future generations?

God will always protect His people. We are the family of God and we are called to live as one, regardless of what life brings. When we are faithful and obey His law, rivers of grace and protection are poured out upon us. So let us unite and work together as a powerful army of love and humility, in one spirit with Christ, as a family that witnesses to the Faith.

As the family of God, we must unite in prayer. As the Servant of God, Father Patrick Peyton, who became known as 'the Rosary Priest' so memorably put it, "The family that prays together stays together". It is important that we live a sacramental life of prayer and become active in parish life because this gives young people a sense of belonging to their church community, even if many of their contemporaries are not enthusiastic about prayer and the Church. The fact that their parents lovingly insist on the Faith, and the religious traditions that keeps them united, marks their future forever and gives them the foundation on which to build their lives. It is for us to lay the foundations.

The greatest enemy of peace today is a family without God. It becomes the nest of all sorts of evil. Within the godless family, the seeds of decadence and immorality are germinated and spread to the whole human family. A family without God is the cradle of divorce, abortion, pornography, alcoholism, drug addiction, homosexuality and lesbianism. It is a factory of dysfunction in which all of society's sickness originates.

The people of God must unite in carefully selecting our political leaders. These policy makers greatly influence families and determine many aspects of our lives through the laws that they implement. Society's values are often a reflection of our leaders' values, morality and state of obedience, or disobedience, to God. They can affect a whole generation, or many generations, for good or evil. We are responsible for electing them. If we fail to participate in elections, our unexercised vote gives a silent vote to those supporting evil policies and agendas and for this we are also responsible.

As Catholics, we have the duty to ensure that we are fully aware of the repercussions of our action in the life of the Church and the family. As the people of God, we have been chosen to be responsible for the whole of humanity. Mystically speaking, a Catholic who lives a faithful matrimonial life is an inspiration for future families and an example for those who do not know God. A married couple inspires hope in the young person who goes to Mass on Sunday who may still be searching for his or her identity and vocation. A happily married couple is a breath of fresh air for the parish priest and an inspiration for bishops in their pastoral work for the family.

We have to build the Church in our homes. We must live our discipleship at home and at work, on the street and in the park, at funerals and at weddings. We are the domestic Church. The family manifests itself and lives the communal nature of the Church as children of God. Each family member, in keeping with his own role, exercises Baptismal priesthood and contributes to making the family a community of grace and prayer, a school of human and Christian virtue, and the place where the Faith is proclaimed for the first time to the children.

The sacrament of Matrimony is the most precious jewel of society. It is the dwelling place of angels and the joy of saints. It is also the greatest nightmare for the spirits of evil. We are living in difficult times. Immorality is celebrated everywhere. Hatred and deception and greed dominate our politicians' lives and policies. Still, we will always have God, who is our strength. No one can separate us from His love and protection. So we will soldier on, living sacramental lives of prayer and holiness, continuing to battle for the salvation of the souls of our brothers and sisters who throw themselves into the enemy's arms with such cheerful indifference.

The Sacramentals

The Catechism tells us:

The sacramentals are sacred signs instituted by the Church to sanctify circumstances of spiritual life, such as the sign of the cross to begin prayer. Among the sacramentals that have an important place are the blessings, which are praises to God and a prayer to receive his gifts, the consecration of individuals and the dedication of objects for the adoration of God. (See Catechism 1667 -1668)

Sacramentals are an essential part of exorcism, which is carried out in its simple form at Baptism. A solemn exorcism, or *great* exorcism, however, is a much more sophisticated ritual and can only be carried out by a bishop or duly appointed priest.

What is an exorcism?

"When the Church asks publicly and authoritatively in the name of Jesus Christ that a person or object be protected against the power of the Evil One and withdrawn from his dominion, it is called exorcism."

(Catechism 1673)

What forms of popular piety accompany the sacramental life of the Church?

"The religious sense of the Christian people has always found expression in various forms of piety surrounding the Church's sacramental life, such as the veneration of relics, visits to sanctuaries, pilgrimages, processions, the stations of the cross, religious dances, the rosary, medals, etc."

(Catechism 1674)

The Church looks favorably upon authentic forms of popular piety and sheds the light of faith on them. This is often an area of major disagreement between 'progressive theologians' and 'traditional, faithful Catholics'. *Sacramentals* present such a scandal to 'modernist clergy' that they will sometimes refuse to use, bless or prepare them for the people. Only the spirit of Satan is tormented by sacramentals. These weapons, properly used, can make a real difference in the daily spiritual battle of all Christians against the forces of evil. Therefore, they should be widely used and promoted in the Church.

While it is true that a poor understanding of sacramentals can lead to superstition, idolatry and fanaticism, the Faith of the Church, and Sacred Tradition, teach us to use sacramentals properly in the fight against Satan. Used appropriately, sacramentals are lethal spiritual weapons.

When the believer understands their power, is in a state of grace, and is faithful to God, sacramentals such as blessed water, oil, candles, rosaries, exorcized salt, medals and images of the saints, the angels and the Blessed Virgin, become the most devastating weapons against evil.

A crucifix that is worn as a necklace, for instance, is not simply a religious object depicting the Crucified. Because the spirits of evils that roam the air live in eternity, they are not subject to time and space as we are. In God's *Eternal Present*, Jesus is on the cross at Golgotha. If the one wearing this sacramental is in a state of grace, and has full knowledge of the power of the sacramental worn, every evil spirit that approaches him will be instantly in the presence of Jesus crucified, not simply in front of a religious object.

The spiritual force of sacramentals lies in one's inner understanding of them. The believer must be totally conscious of their meaning in relation to the spiritual battle. In other words, the use of a sacramental should not have, as its sole purpose, the power to protect. It must also be available as a weapon for combating evil in all circumstances.

Separated Christians generally have a poor understanding of sacramentals, especially sacred images. Regarding the use of religious objects, images and statues in sacred history, they are confused about the interpretation of the Word of God in the transition between the Old and New Testaments.

When the Catholic clergy lose respect for popular piety and dismiss sacramentals, considering them worthless or an embarrassment, this is a sure sign of an undernourished priesthood and an indication that the priest is in serious spiritual danger. It belies a spiritual arrogance and pride. In many cases the action of evil will already have taken hold in that priest. God has created a Church and His Holy Spirit has journeyed with His people inspiring them to express their faith in symbols and images that describe the times of earthly pilgrimage from generation to generation. When we turn our backs on these and criticize them as idolatry or useless tradition, we are separating ourselves from the rhythm of salvation, ignoring the signs of the times and failing to appreciate the precious spiritual seasons of God's providence. We are trampling on His beautiful saving work with His People. We must not erase Sacred Tradition or ignore the tracks of the pilgrimage of the people of God, because these tracks, this Tradition, is our story and an essential part of our identity as the people of God.

The Catholic Funeral

The Catechism describes the relationship between the sacraments and the destiny of the Christian soul as follows:

> All the sacraments, and principally those of Christian initiation, have as their goal the last Passover of the child of God which, through death, leads him into the life of the Kingdom. Then what he confessed in faith and hope will be fulfilled: "I look for the resurrection of the dead, and the life of the world to come." (Niceno-Constantinopolitan Creed).
>
> (Catechism 1680)

The Christian, who dies in Christ, attains, at the end of his earthly life, the fulfillment of the new life that began with Baptism. He is strengthened in Confirmation and nourished in the Eucharist, the foretaste of the heavenly banquet.The meaning of a Christian's death is made evident in the Death and Resurrection of Christ, our only hope. The Christian, who dies in Jesus Christ, prefers to "be away from the body and at home with the Lord" (2 Cor. 5:8).

When the soul is separated from the body, it enters the fullness of the spiritual world and is immediately confronted with the reality of the spirits of darkness that inhabit this world. The extent to which a soul is capable of defending itself will depend on how strong the soul is. A weak soul that has lived only according to the laws of the flesh and the world, is greatly undernourished and will lack the strength to be able to pass through the low spiritual world and into the light. If, owing to the mercy of God, this soul is granted salvation at the last moment, it will remain in a difficult state of purification in Purgatory, where its only desire will be to ascend to the heights of light, and to God.

A faithful Christian soul, however, is able to immediately attain the plenitude of light at the moment of death and passes, with spiritual authority, through the lower spiritual realm, to the Kingdom of Light. As this will be its last ever encounter with the forces of evil, the soul will have to engage in a tremendous battle, even if it be the soul of the greatest saint. At the moment of death, evil attacks the soul with its severest temptations, accusing it of its past, and uses all its power to make the soul feel unworthy to fly to God. The devil uses every weapon at his disposal against that soul, even when he knows that the soul belongs to God. The one who dies in friendship with God is covered with divine protection, is filled with wisdom and will not delay in exercising authority over the spirits of darkness. It will fly victorious to the Heavenly Jerusalem.

The Church constantly reminds us of the importance of preparing for a good death and invoking Saint Joseph as a powerful advocate for that very moment. The Church also recommends devotion to the holy angels, especially the Archangel St Michael who plays a vital role in the final battle for the soul's salvation.

The spiritual growth which we achieve during this life is the stairway by which we ascend to God. How much we have grown in the spirit determines the precise height of our stairway at the moment of death. The bottom line is, if we have really learned to love God and our neighbor unconditionally, we will attain the Kingdom of God the instant we die.

Our relationship with the Virgin Mary is a colossal tower of blinding light in the lower realm of spirits. Our Mother Mary represents a spiritual economy that has grown richer and richer through the centuries. Her presence represents the maternal protection of the womb of the Church and is a reminder of the womb of this simple, humble Jewish woman, where Christian life began with the Incarnation of the Lord Jesus. Placed in her womb was the *Source of Eternal Life*, the Redeemer of the whole human race. An ordinary human being was the recipient of the Holy Spirit. Mary helps us to build our faith in the realm of the chosen ones of God. If we accept this mystery, we will be able to embrace it in its fullness and develop a holy relationship with the maternity of the Church.

A Catholic funeral is Mother Church's preparation of a soul for its presentation before the Heavenly Court. It is the moment when Mother Church nudges one of her children out of the nest when its time comes to fly home to God. When we are faithful to God and we die in Christ, to die means to live eternally. The physical body is buried but the soul lives on and awaits the resurrection of the dead.

As Christians, we know that, at the Last Judgment, our physical bodies will be returned to us in a state of perfection and immortality. This is, in itself, a cause of great of joy for those of us who live in the hope of the promise of Christ, Our Lord.

The Vocation of Man: Life in the Spirit

When we speak of 'Life in the Spirit', we are concerned with man's call to penetrate the mysteries of the faith in a mystical sense. It is precisely the failure to strive for this 'Life in the Spirit' that has led to the decline in the Church's numbers in recent years. We are spiritually ill-prepared for the times we are facing. Much confusion reigns in our spiritual territories. Instead of defending them, as we ought, we actually seem to be quite receptive to the *Demonic Invader's* poisonous proposals. It is a sad spectacle indeed to see the *People of God* so lamentably weakened. We need to strengthen the life of faith, our lives in the Spirit, through sacramental means.

The Catechism describes the link between the Christian moral life to faith and the sacraments. What is signified by the symbols of the faith is communicated through the sacraments. Through the sacraments, the faithful receive the grace of Christ and the gifts of the Holy Spirit, furnishing them with the capacity to live a new life as children of God in Christ. What great dignity is ours. "O Christian, know your dignity", Saint Leo the Great exhorts us.

The Catechism tells us:

> The dignity of the human person is rooted in his creation in the image and likeness of God; it is fulfilled in his vocation to divine beatitude.
>
> (Catechism 1700)

> Endowed with a spiritual soul, with intellect and with free will, the human person is from his very conception ordered to God and destined for eternal beatitude. He pursues his perfection in "seeking and loving what is true and good".
>
> (Catechism 1711)

We can attain happiness in virtue of the grace of Christ, who makes us participants in the divine life. In the Gospel, Christ points out to his followers the way that leads to eternal happiness, the Beatitudes. The grace of Christ is also operative in all persons who, with right conscience, seek and love truth and goodness, and avoid evil. (See Catechism 1716-1719).

Eternal happiness is the vision of God in eternal life in which we are "participants of the divine nature" (2 Pet. 1:4), of the glory of Christ and of the joy of the Trinitarian life. This happiness exceeds any human capacity. It is a supernatural and free gift of God, that comes from grace. This happiness sustains us during difficult moments, challenging moral choices and worldly affairs. It urges us on to love God above all things.

To really try to be good, and faithful to God, is to choose a path of sanctity. We begin to live a holy life when everything we do is centered on pleasing God. This will inevitably entail battling with ourselves because human nature naturally tends to the things of the flesh. With the help of grace, however, we are able to direct this tendency towards the Spirit. When we do this, we begin a real voyage to the soul's home, the eternal abode in the glory of God. We are free to act, or not to act, in every situation. We have received our *freedom* from God and we are responsible for our own deliberate actions. The more good we do, the more free we become. It is a basic rule in the *economy of salvation* that we must constantly live according to what is good, so that we can advance towards the territory of light. (For further reflection, see the Catechism, paragraphs 1699-1700 and 1720-1748).

The Nature of Sin

The Catechism tells us:

> Sin is an offence against reason, truth and right cons-
> cience; it is failure in genuine love for God and neigh-
> bor caused by a perverse attachment to certain goods.
> It wounds the nature of man and injures human soli-
> darity. It has been defined as 'an utterance, a deed or a
> desire contrary to the eternal law'.
>
> (Catechism 1849)

In his Passion, Christ reveals fully the gravity of sin and
overcomes it with His compassion. If we know the gravity of
the consequences of sin, our responsibility not to remain enslaved to it enormously increases. Our life is a constant state
of growth towards abandoning the material for the spiritual.
God has revealed the way to us in Jesus Christ, His Son, in
whom we must walk. We must leave what is evil to keep to the
spiritual path of God.

Is there a diversity of sins?

> Sins can be distinguished according to their objects, as
> can every human act; or according to the virtues they
> oppose, by excess or defect, or according to the com-

mandments they violate. They can also be classed according to whether they concern God, neighbor or oneself; they can be divided into spiritual and carnal sins, or again as sins in thought, word, deed or omission.

(Catechism 1853)

How are sins distinguished according to their gravity?

A distinction is made between mortal and venial sin. (See Catechism 1854-1864).

When is a mortal sin committed?

A mortal sin is committed when there co-exist: grave matter, full knowledge and deliberate consent. This sin destroys charity in us, deprives us of sanctifying grace, and, if there is no repentance, leads us to eternal death in hell. It can be forgiven in the ordinary way through the sacraments of Baptism and Confession. (See Catechism 1263, 1857-1861)

When is a venial sin committed?

One commits venial sin when, in a less serious matter, one does not observe the standard prescribed by the moral law, or when one disobeys the moral law in a grave matter, but without full knowledge or without complete consent.

Venial sin weakens charity; it manifests a disordered affection for created goods; it impedes the soul's progress in the exercise of virtues and the practice of the moral good; it merits temporal punishment. Deliberate and unrepented venial sin disposes us little by little to commit mortal sin. However venial sin does not set us in direct opposition to the will and friendship of God; it does not break the covenant with God. With God's grace it is humanly reparable. 'Venial sin does not deprive the sinner of sanctifying grace, friendship with God, charity, and consequently eternal happiness.' (John Paul II, RP 17 # 9)

> While he is in the flesh, man cannot help but have at least some light sins. But do not despise these sins which we call 'light': if you take them for light when you weigh them, tremble when you count them. A number of light objects makes a great mass; a number of drops fills a river; a number of grains makes a heap. What then is our hope? Above all, confession ...
>
> (Catechism 1862 & 1863)

Today there is a basic ignorance regarding *sin*. Millions come into this life and are not taught anything about God, or the need to honor, love and obey Him. The word sin has been reduced to a philosophical concept, an abstract notion, nothing really worth bothering about.

How can the idea of sin be understood, though, if God is not known, if one has no concept of having been created or any sense that obedience may be due to something greater than one's instincts and reason? We live in a world in which the vast majority of people believe only in themselves. This alone creates a vacuum, devoid of the love of God, which turns life into sin. The result is a perverted, decadent and aggressively secular world.

We must take care, however, not to judge anyone else. Each of us is the result of our upbringing, our background and the generations that came before us. We must be conscious of this and begin to act now to break these chains of misery and spiritual blindness that binds our brothers and sisters so tightly.

Who is going to pave the way for future generations? Is anyone at all concerned about this? If we are going to embrace the fullness of our responsibility as Christians, we must present the Faith by living authentic Christian lives. This will be a true witness. Someone has to dare to stand up for holiness. We are all called to be columns of light for this world. Priests are becoming so weak spiritually, that some consider celibacy to be optional. There is little understanding of the importance and the spiritual nature of the vows of poverty and obedience.

What is the moral law and in what does it consist?

The moral law is a work of divine wisdom. In it are established the forms and rules of conduct that lead to the promised happiness, and prohibit the ways that distance us from God. (See Catechism 1959-1978)

The natural moral law, inscribed by the Creator on the heart of each person, consists of participation in the wisdom and goodness of God. It expresses the original moral sense that enables one to discern, through reason, *good* and *evil*. It is universal and immutable and it also determines the basis of the fundamental rights and duties of a person.

As Catholics, we know that salvation is for everyone. The fact that every human being is born with the natural law inscribed in his heart means that God wants us all to know Him, to obey Him and to love Him. He wants us all to attain the eternal abode of His glory.

This shows the responsibility that we have towards the rest of humanity. To be a Catholic is not a condition for salvation. To be a Catholic is to have been enrolled in the most powerful army, for the salvation of souls.

How does the Church nourish the moral life of the Christian?

The Church is the community in which the Christian receives the Word of God, the teachings of the "Law of Christ" (Gal. 6:2) and the grace of the sacraments. Christians are united with the Eucharistic Sacrifice of Christ in such a way that their moral life is an act of spiritual adoration. They learn the example of holiness from the Virgin Mary and the life of the saints. (See Catechism 2030, 2031)

Why does the Magisterium of the Church act in the field of morality?

It is the responsibility of the Church's Magisterium to preach the Faith which must be believed and put into practice in our lives. This duty extends also to the specific precepts of the natural law, because their observance is also necessary for salvation. (See Catechism 2032-2051)

It is apparent, however, that many pay no heed to the precepts of the Church, nor to the precepts of natural law, preferring to gallop headlong into disobedience, immorality and disaster rather than steadily walking the path to Eternal Life guided by the sound doctrine of the Gospel.

Virtues

It is a serious challenge to even attempt to introduce the subject of virtue to people today. It seems that everything in modern society directly opposes the very idea of virtue. Modernists are scandalized when they see the faithful being led on this path. In many cases, religion has become a relic of the past, a chapter in human history beyond which we need to progress. The concept of virtue today is reserved solely for describing the talented individual or the one who is especially meticulous at his trade. No longer do we speak of virtue when referring to the moral human being living in obedience to God's Commandments.

I believe that one needs to cultivate a virtuous life in order to live coherently within the spiritual order of things. If we are not walking on this path of morals, we will simply become dysfunctional, unreliable people who cannot be trusted even in the most basic things in life. People who are not virtuous are simply worldly, materialistic and superficial. How can I do good if I do not know what it is and have never cultivated the good habit of loving my neighbor? This lack of love alone will reduce any possibility of enduring relationships and sincere communication with others because I will only be focused on myself. This is typically the case where there is an absence of virtue.

According to the Catechism:

> A virtue is an habitual and firm disposition to do the good. It allows the person not only to perform good acts, but to give the best of himself. ... The goal of a virtuous life is to become like God.
>
> (Catechism 1803)

There are human and theological virtues:

Human Virtues

> Human virtues are firm attitudes, stable dispositions and habitual perfections of intellect and will that govern our actions, order our passions and guide our conduct according to reason and faith.
>
> (Catechism 1804)

They are acquired and strengthened by the repetition of morally good acts and are purified and elevated by divine grace. The principal human virtues are called "cardinal virtues". They are: prudence, justice, fortitude and temperance.

Theological Virtues

> The human virtues are rooted in the theological virtues, which adapt man's faculties for participation in the divine nature: for the theological virtues relate directly to God. They dispose Christians to live in a relationship with the Holy Trinity. They have the One and Triune God for their origin, motive and object. The theological virtues are the foundation of Christian moral activity; they animate it and give it its special character. They in-

form and give life to all the moral virtues. They are infused by God into the souls of the faithful to make them
capable of acting as His children and of meriting eternal
life. They are the pledge of the presence and action of
the Holy Spirit in the faculties of the human being. There are three theological virtues: faith, hope and charity
(cf. 1 Cor. 13:13).

(Catechism 1812 -1813)

In order to fulfill the task of being in God, living according to
His will, we must know how to operate within the Church,
and this is only possible through the action of the Holy Spirit.

What are the gifts of the Holy Spirit?

The moral life of Christians is sustained by the gifts of the
Holy Spirit. These are permanent dispositions which make
man docile in following the promptings of the Holy Spirit.

The seven gifts of the Holy Spirit are wisdom, understanding, counsel, fortitude, knowledge, piety, and fear of the Lord.
They belong in their fullness to Christ, Son of David (Isa. 11:1-
2). They complete and perfect the virtues of those who receive
them. They make the faithful docile in readily obeying divine
inspirations.

> "Let your good spirit lead me on a level path." (Ps
> 143:10). For all who are led by the Spirit of God are sons
> of God... If children, then heirs, heirs of God and fellow
> heirs with Christ." (Rom. 8:14-17).

(Catechism 1830 - 1831)

What are the fruits of the Holy Spirit?

> The fruits of the Holy Spirit are perfections that the Holy Spirit forms in us as the first fruits of eternal glory. The tradition of the Church lists twelve of them: 'charity, joy, peace, patience, kindness, goodness, generosity, gentleness, faithfulness, modesty, self-control, chastity'. (Gal. 5:22-23)
>
> (Catechism 1832)

The outward signs of someone who is sincerely walking with God and living according to these steps of spiritual growth are simple and powerful. It is plain to see that this person is free of the slavery of materialism and is above the slavery of instinct, disordered passions and of rationalism. This is truly *Life in the Spirit,* where peace has been reached and where internal areas of human weakness have been overcome. This brings order and coherence and establishes a solid foundation upon which a true edifice of faith can be raised.

Spiritual Growth

Spiritual growth requires a docility of heart to allow the Holy Spirit to act on the gifts given to the soul at Baptism. It is the building of our eternal salvation on the foundation which is Christ himself in his Church, making use of all He taught us through the apostles.

Priests and religious who are not strong because they lack spirituality, who are not strong in prayer and live a dissolute life, will fall as ripe fruit falls from a tree. These are times in which the *Forces of Darkness* are at their highest level of activity against the whole of humanity. A person consecrated to God is the greatest object of Evil's attack, because he can deprive them of strength and power to act against the people of God. A humble and holy priest, or a faithful consecrated religious, is the real presence of the living Christ in our midst. In fact, God floods such individuals with the most astonishing gifts during their lives. They will be instruments of salvation for thousands of souls. They are true souls of reparation.

We must all be Saints if we are to live the fruits of the Holy Spirit, and this means becoming very little, so little that we become absolutely insignificant to those around us who are not spiritual. We become bread without yeast, insipid to the palates of the world. Spiritual growth restores the purity and innocence that has been lost to sin.

Prayer

We could fill hundreds of volumes of the richest theology but, without a significant consideration of the importance of prayer, these would be wholly-lacking, impoverished treatments on the essence of the knowledge of God.

Prayer is the raising of one's mind and heart to God or the petition of good things from Him, according to his will. It is always a gift of God, the well where Christ comes to meet those seeking water. Prayer is the encounter of God's thirst with ours. The prayer of a Christian is the essential, personal relationship of a child of God with the Father, who is infinitely good, with his Son Jesus Christ and with the Holy Spirit, who dwells in his heart. (See Catechism 2559-2560)

There is a universal call to prayer in the act of creation. God calls every being from nothingness into existence. Even after *the* Fall, man continues to be able to recognize his Creator and maintains the desire for the One who called him into existence. All religions and histories of salvation attest, in particular, to this human desire for God. It is God, in the first place, who tirelessly calls each person to that mysterious encounter known as prayer. (See Catechism 2566-2567)

Abraham is a model of prayer because he walked in the presence of God, listened to him and obeyed him. His prayer was a battle of faith, because he continued to believe in God's fidelity, even in times of trial. He receives the Lord in his tent, and God reveals his plan for him. Abraham also intercedes for sinners with bold confidence. (See Catechism 2568 - 2572)

What is the role of prayer in the mission of the prophets?

The prophets drew light and strength from prayer to exhort the people to faith and heartfelt conversion. They entered into great intimacy with God and interceded for their brothers and sisters to whom they proclaimed what they had seen and heard from the Lord. Elijah was the father of prophets, of those who seek God's face. On Mount Carmel he succeeded in obtaining God's intervention, praying: "Answer me, O Lord, answer me!" (1 Kgs. 18:37). (See Catechism 2582- 2583)

How did Moses pray? Moses' prayer is typical of contemplative prayer. God, who called Moses from the burning bush, often spoke at length to him, "face to face, as a man speaks to his friend" (Exod. 33:11). In his intimacy with God, Moses gained the strength to intercede steadfastly for his people, so much so, that he prefigured the prayer of intercession of the one Mediator, Christ Jesus. (See Catechism 2574-2576)

Prayer was revealed and fully realized in Jesus. With His human heart, Jesus learned the formulas of prayer from His mother and from the Jewish tradition. However, His prayer rose from a more secret source, because He is the Eternal Son of God, who, in His holy humanity, offers His perfect filial prayer to His Father. (See Catechism 2599)

When Jesus prays, He is already teaching us how to pray. His prayer to His Father is the theological path (the path of faith, hope and charity) of our prayer to God.

(Catechism 2607)

Thus, in addition to the content, he teaches us the necessary disposition for true prayer: a purity of heart that seeks the kingdom and forgives enemies; bold and filial faith that goes beyond what we feel and understand; and vigilance, which protects the disciple from temptation.
(See Catechism 2607-2612)

The Virgin Mary's prayer was characterized by faith and by the generous offer of her whole being to God. Jesus' mother is also the new Eve, "Mother of all the living" (Gen. 3:20). She prays to Jesus for the needs of the whole people. By having a relationship with God, one has a supernatural life. Prayer is the presence of the living God in our hearts. We will not be able to pray if God is not in our heart. Thus, the beginning of prayer is found in the movement of God's Spirit towards the human creature. It is a magnificent act of true love which leads to greater knowledge of God's mysterious ways. So, when we pray we have already received grace, and the Holy Spirit dwells in the depth of our heart.

Once prayer is established as a spiritual language - regardless of how simple, humble or basic it might be - and we completely surrender our earthly lives into God's hands, then, through the supernatural grace this pours into our hearts, our natural life becomes a real anointing for humanity.

In the Old Testament, it was only the prophets chosen by God who interceded directly before him. Thus we see Levi's priests interceding for their own sins and those of the people. However, their effectiveness cannot be compared with that of the prophets. Now we have Jesus Christ and our prayers go directly to Him, and from Him, directly to the Father. Saint Paul prays, "May the God of peace make you holy and bring you to perfection. May you be completely blameless, in spirit, soul and body, till the coming of Christ Jesus, our Lord" (1 Thess. 5:23).

This commitment can only be achieved if one is completely immersed in God's Holy Spirit, through a life of constant prayer. We must be spiritual always, and not just for religious reasons, on occasions when we are in need, or on traditional occasions when the sacraments and religious feasts are celebrated.

Once the soul is anchored in Christ through sincere and persevering prayer, it wants to stay in that intimacy and that unity will free his whole being. Prayer is a movement of the soul that unites us to the Sacred Heart of Jesus. Once this union is obtained, prayer becomes the oxygen of the spiritual life.

There is an immense treasure in prayer which is not exploited enough. If we only knew the transcendental change that takes place in our hearts once the soul enters the chamber of God's silence and penetrates the infinite kingdom of His love and compassion, we would not hesitate a moment but would direct our whole being to that end.

Prayer is peace which brings joy and freedom. Prayer means having the supernatural unction of the company of the angels and saints, an intimate relationship with the Virgin Mary and access to the treasures of the spiritual kingdom of the *Church Triumphant* in heaven. When we are united in prayer, we become an unconquerable power against evil. Then, we walk in the light and blind the spirits of darkness.

The silence that envelops the soul once it has received the gift of prayer is so precious, that the whole being is transformed into a new life, where the only longing is for more silence, more peace, more freedom. It is a holy adhesion of divine dependence. (For further reading on the prayer of the Blessed Virgin Mary, see Catechism 1619 and 2617).

What are the sources of Christian prayer? They are: the Word of God that gives us "the surpassing worth of knowing Christ Jesus" (Phil. 3:8); the Liturgy of the Church that proclaims, makes present and communicates the mystery of Salvation; the theological virtues and all daily situations, as we can find God in them. (See Catechism 2652-2660)

Emanating from the depth of the human heart is the need to get to the core of the soul, to reach God the Creator. It is a natural need. It is the reason and source of all levels of spiritual seeking. In the midst of this search, and despite their sincerity, human beings often end up contemplating the *Kingdom of Spiritual Darkness*. Great dangers may then arise which can prove fatal for some souls.

It is common to find a growing hunger for spiritual food, partly as a consequence of the materialism that surrounds us. Regardless of its spiritual state, the soul needs just as much regular nourishment as the physical body. The devil is prompt to supply false nourishment, using all possible ways to satisfy human expectations, taking into account their cultures, idio-syncrasies and different social, economic and political states, etc.

Prayer protects the faithful from the deceit of the world. The spiritual language of the times is always challenging for the faithful to discern. The devil always replicates and misrep-resents the truth. The counterfeiting is so convincing, that, if the faithful are not properly formed in their faith, or are un-faithful to God, they can be easily deceived by the Evil One.

Today, the deceptions present themselves in the human sci-ences through Eastern philosophies, humanist psychology, mental control techniques, and so many different forms of the occult and fortune telling. The options for idolatry offered by Satan are limitless: the worship of idols, money and fame; ce-lebrity, information technology, etc.

The power of prayer keeps one steady in the midst of all this deceit and conquers the territory of light, the realm of the spir-its of God where there is joy and freedom. A Catholic should have an assiduous life of prayer; prayer must become second nature, a spontaneous internal activity of the heart and soul, as natural as breathing. It is a source of strength that will give us a thirst for a sacramental life. We long to always be recon-ciled with God, to be a faithful friend of the Most High. We hunger for the *Bread of Life*, the flesh and blood of the Lamb: *The Holy Eucharist*.

The *Forces of Evil* are blocked by the prayers of the faithful. They are consumed by the fire of the Holy Spirit who reigns in the heart of those who pray. How powerful is the action of prayer when the heart is one with God! It is a powerful weapon against evil.

What is lacking in the Catholic Church today is a true life of prayer. We must reclaim the contemplative life of the liturgy, which is the true incense of prayer. Parishes today tend to be filled with the noise of the world instead of the silence of God. They end up by bringing the world to God's temple. It is very common to see parishes that have become excellent social clubs, immersed in great works of charity and numerous ministries, but completely devoid of prayer and spirituality.

Prayer is the source of vocations, the inspiration of young generations, the hope of adults and the strength of the elderly. It is an infinite source of blessings, and it is Jesus himself who gave us the example when he withdrew alone to the mountain to pray to his heavenly Father.

Prayer is Jesus resurrecting Lazarus, it is Jesus in Gethsemane, it is Jesus walking the Via Dolorosa to Golgotha. Prayer is the most wonderful gift that unites us intimately with God. It is Jesus agonizing on the cross. Prayer is Mary, John and the holy women of Jerusalem living Jesus' agony at the foot of the Cross. It is Mary Magdalene rising early to care for her Lord's body on the morning of the Resurrection.

Prayer is the profound faith of the martyrs throughout the centuries. It is the powerful mystery of the Most Holy Rosary of the Blessed Virgin Mary. Prayer is all the mysteries of our Faith that nourish our conversation with God and inspire us to proclaim Him to all.

Interior Silence

In a world where noise completely dominates our urban living, we should be careful that our own personal din does not add to the general cacophony.

If we do not keep guard over our senses, we are in danger of being taken over by the very things that our senses are perceiving. We see the effects of this all around us. Millions depend on medication for depression and many other illnesses where the causes have not been identified. Human science will never be able to cope with all the physical and mental sicknesses we see in the world today.

We often act through our senses, unaware of the impact they have on us, for good or for evil. We are educated to focus our senses directly on a physical objective without ever understanding the repercussions it has on our inner being. For instance, every time we concentrate on hearing a certain sound, we open our mind to it, allowing it to penetrate our interior and to affect us according to its nature. Our mind distributes the sound according to the sensations it produces in our whole being. When we listen to music, for instance, we receive sonic 'commands' which influence thought and behavior. These sound waves also penetrate the mind, the center of one's being, accessing areas that are generally not easily reached. The intensity and speed of musical sounds can affect everything from the digestive system to the smallest nerve of the body, depending on the rhythm and levels of electronic or acoustic waves.

Certain sounds activate chemical substances in the body which do not necessarily correspond to a natural equilibrium of the organism and so may upset the general balance of health. However, even when we are exposed to sound, it will not be fully active in our interior if we are not completely receptive to it and do not give it our full attention. Then the active sound will only affect us minimally, at a superficial level.

We can be in a place filled with sound and clamorous noise and still be able to isolate ourselves psychologically and emotionally from it all through our will. Our being is more sophisticated than we know. It has been supernaturally anointed by the Holy Spirit through the sacraments. It is extraordinarily prudent in its capacity to discern what it should assimilate and what is should filter out.

The same principle applies to visual perception. What we see affects our entire physical system. If we see something pleasant, it animates our whole being, creating feelings of peace. If we see something disagreeable, it disturbs our whole organism and leaves us disturbed. Audio-visual sensations also stimulate the memory and arouse feelings and emotions. The senses of taste and smell, too, can also trigger memories and associations.

Our senses are so effective at *reading* our external environment that they will register everything that is located in our immediate vicinity. Once scanned and recognized as something associated with the stored memory, our mind enters a state of acceptance and relaxes. These sensory occurrences create impulses or reactions. These may be foreseen or unforeseen. They may be positive or negative depending on how we have been affected by what we have perceived.

When, for example, what is *read* by the senses does not correspond to what the memory determines to be familiar, the mind can be seized by insecurity or fear. When we see something which the brain recognizes as familiar, or pleasant, then the pleasure centers of the brain are stimulated.

We are not going to enjoy a well-balanced, healthy life unless our basic human nature that is subjugated to these physical laws is restrained by the Spirit. Humanity today lives according to its lower instincts and is focused solely on satisfying primitive human desires and base urges. This is why we are falling deeper and deeper into extreme materialism. We are a very weak human race that is unable to cope with the pressures of the daily demands of the industrialized world we have created to aid our survival. We have forgotten something important. Human beings are not the manufactured product of human hands. Our survival requires more than that which the external world alone can give us.

The greatest cry of Heaven is the immense need for *evangelization*. The materialistic rationalism of our civilization claims ever more victims. Mortality rates are greatly exceeding birth rates in many countries in the world today. This is a really great evil of our time.

It is essential to embrace a high spiritual discipline and to begin to fight for what is 'of the spirit'. We must begin serious preparation in order to become true spiritual beings. The spiritual formation of the senses is vital if we are to begin to strengthen our whole being. Everything that surrounds us needs to be carefully sifted with consideration given as to how such things may affect or influence us.

If we wish to be strong, we must abandon the works of the flesh, and embrace those of the spirit. In order to achieve a true interior silence, and health of body, mind and soul, we must be masters of our whole being, and subject ourselves to total obedience to the spirit.

How can the senses be formed spiritually? The sense of sight operates without much discrimination. The state of innocence of many children is lost through this sense. One might argue that it is impossible to avoid. How can one prevent a child looking at something he shouldn't? No one can have complete control over a child's visual activity. However, it is possible to keep him away from images that may sully his innocence, such as television, video games and the internet. These precautions make it possible to diminish the initial risk protecting his interior health. I am not speaking of concupiscence of the eyes in this case, as a child will not yet have that awareness of sin; however, if he is not properly protected, this may develop prematurely.

Having lived our entire lives unaware of the importance of cultivating a strict discipline of the senses, we may begin to understand its importance for spiritual growth. We start by taking small steps. The first practical step is to learn to be more discriminating with regard to the potentially harmful audio-visuals that confront us. Learning to keep our eyes fixed in one direction will help us to control what we take in. This is no easy task but, with perseverance, we will soon develop a more disciplined management of our sense of sight. This brings a definite peace to heart and soul.

If we focus on doing this with every one of our senses, we will begin to have control of the flesh and find ourselves on the way to a new life. It will be easy to enter the Kingdom of the Spirit and we will bear fruit in abundance. These will be the lasting fruits of true love, peace and charity. Then we will enter, finally, into the silence of God.

The main victory is the ability to be able to live in the present. Once we succeed in really focusing on the moment, our whole being enters a state of harmony. We will not suffer anxiety, emptiness or sensations of loneliness and depression. When we are not focused on 'the now', on the present moment, our lives are dispersed and unfocused and we live in a vacuum that cannot be filled. Not to live in the present moment is to die in time. In other words, it is to live absent, it is not to exist according to spiritual laws, and the result is the disturbance of physical laws. This, in turn, affects our physical and mental health and brings the loss of interior silence.

Mastery of one's senses represents a triumph over the flesh and a victory of the soul. Our physical nature is a precious gift. It is the foundation of a life that transcends the present temporarily, to the extent that we understand that we are part of a reality that goes beyond what is physical and tangible. We are able to profit from our spiritual growth each second of our existence. This enables us to find true freedom, true peace and true joy to carry out the mission for which God created us.

We must understand how vital it is to have a life totally focused on the here and now. This is necessary to be really effective. Day dreaming only works when we have no need to focus or when we are taking a moment of rest. An Air Force pilot flying a combat plane at high speed is unlikely to spend a second unfocused. Living is like flying a combat plane at great speed. We are facing enemies of the soul that live in an *eternal present*, outside of time and space. If we are not conscious of this fact, we can be dragged down by those forces which move instantaneously. The only way that we can be protected, from all that threatens to destroy us, is by being faithful to God. Then we will not be afraid. We will be safe, astute and ready to fight evil.

It is essential that we strive for interior silence. This is only attained with the peace that the Holy Spirit brings to His faithful people. When we succeed in living a life in obedience to God, despite having lived our life primarily in exile, we will sail through storms and darkness. Though unable to see our destiny on the horizon, we are certain that Jesus, our captain, is with us and that we will reach the port safely. Despite everything, we will not be afraid, and nothing will be able to separate us from His love (Rom. 8:38-39).

It is for this reason that a high degree of discipline is needed. We must become very strong spiritually if we are to rescue those who are trapped and lost in an abyss of emptiness, with no ears to hear and no eyes to see. (Mark. 4:12).

Only God can give us such a grace. We are His instruments. Where He is, we must be also. He calls us to sow and water His works of love and compassion with the souls entrusted to us each day. God rescues such souls, putting them in a state of rehabilitation, giving them the opportunity for salvation, exactly as He has done with all of us on numerous occasions.

We must really begin to live our new life in Christ, leaving the old ways behind, making ourselves new, walking with God's spirit in our being and feeling that we are finally alive with a true spiritual sense. Let us live with a new conscience that is not obstructed by sin, or eclipsed by doubts, the spirit of curiosity or disobedience to God.

If we are able to maintain these levels of awareness and discipline, our life will become profitable for the *Economy of Salvation* which is nothing other than God's plan for humanity. Then, we will be living in the *Holy Will of God*.

Once all this has occurred, the change will be immense and there will be a total transformation in our way of living and in the way we perceive and conceive our existence. We will be completely new persons. We will have spiritual strength and interior health to forgive our past, to repent sincerely and to change our ways, to learn to truly love and to forgive the offences of all others. This, in itself, is already an infinite ocean of true peace in mind and heart.

Spiritual growth is not a mental control technique. It is not merely an exercise in positive thinking or self-esteem. It is more than this, something beyond science and human knowledge. These can never be sources of true growth. They only help to satisfy a very temporal and superficial state of being. They are only fleeting gains. To grow spiritually is really to travel to the unknown realms of the 'beyond' of God. It is to embrace the plenitude of a reality without end which gives us, even in the midst of the material world, a quality of life that nothing and no one could ever provide. Just being aware of the real conditions, which we must observe, is proof of our spiritual nature. Otherwise, how could we fight what is not flesh and blood, a war that goes beyond human powers, a battle against invisible enemies?

We are approaching Jesus' return. I do not claim to know the exact moment - only God knows that - but one thing is for certain; we are close. The battle with the forces of evil is ever greater, because their time is coming to an end. It is no use knowing the truth if we do not act on it. In order to achieve true silence, we must become spiritual beings. To be able to live a true interior silence, we must turn down the volume of distractions surrounding us. We must simplify every aspect of our daily life.

We are all built on an edifice of pretentiousness. From the beginning of our life, we 'create' a person conditioned to live among others in the natural world. A character, a personality is developed that must be sufficiently strong to allow us to operate in daily life that is often unpredictable. The more adult we are, the larger the world in which we must navigate, and the harder the shell in which we enclose ourselves out of a pure survival instinct.

When we each examine our heart profoundly and unmask this manufactured character, the shell is broken. We find that it is not real; it has replaced the true person. This is a dramatic encounter with an absurd reality. There is only one option once we make this discovery; we must wake up and face the reality of our situation. This is what is known as the beginning of a conversion. This moment, when we genuinely begin to doubt ourselves for the first time, is one of the most significant in any life.

It is a magnificent awakening. One feels one is dying, and at the same time, one experiences the dawn of a long-awaited day. It is the birth of a profound and secret dream, which has waited to flower in a field of a precious spring of the soul. When this happens, the whole world is affected, the whole cosmos is enriched and everything moves towards God. The Mystical Body of Christ is augmented.

Achieving true interior silence does not isolate us from participating in normal life. It places us in a state of serenity which will most certainly also become a source of peace for all those around us. It is the perfect illumination of our conscience.

Modern Theologies

L ike many of the Catholic faithful, I have had the great
misfortune, on several occasions, to hear the preaching
of Sunday homilies that are completely heretical. This is truly lamentable. What is worse is that the experience is made
all the more frustrating because there seems to be no one to
help. No matter how often these matters get reported to the
Church hierarchy, nothing ever seems to be done about it.
This is because, in many cases, the bishops are even more mis-
guided than the priests. The pervasiveness of this false theology is astonishing and Catholics who object to it are labeled
'right-wing' and fundamentalist. Even the priests and bishops
within the Church who hold and preach sound doctrine are
persecuted.

It is reported that during the almost eight years of his pontificate, Pope Benedict XVI suspended a significant number
of bishops from pastoral life - an average of two or three a
month. Many were dismissed from their pastoral functions
and others suspended permanently from their priestly tasks.
Not in vain did this Holy Father serve for twenty-five years as
Prefect of the *Congregation for the Doctrine of the Faith.* He had
profound knowledge of the internal problems of the Church,
where those problems were and who was responsible. Not
only is this good news but also alarming proof of how bad
the state of the Church really is. We hope the Holy Spirit will

inspire Pope Francis to continue his predecessor's great work for the sake of the whole Church and of humanity itself.

We all need to wake up and embrace the responsibility of defending the Church, with which the Lord has entrusted us. We cannot just leave the matter to clergy or religious. We, the laity, have grown so cold and indifferent to our responsibilities in relation to the Church that we no longer inspire young people to consider the priestly or religious life.

Everybody wants a famous doctor, a great lawyer, a distinguished politician, or a millionaire in the family, but not a priest or any other religious or missionary vocation. We are all failing in this regard. It is time to wake up, because if we continue to act like this, we might end up in a painful Purgatory, where we will no longer be able to remedy anything.

One of the greatest and most widespread evils today is that Catholics are no longer going, or being encouraged to go, to confess their sins. This is because, based on the false doctrine they received in seminary, deluded priests declare there to be no such thing as hell or Purgatory or even sin. They are very sadly mistaken. In the United States, lay men and women cannot be leaders in the pastoral life of parishes unless they have a degree in theology or religious sciences. So, it is very common to meet laymen who have the same corrupt theologies as those that have formed the clergy over the last fifty years. Consequently, there are thousands and thousands of American Catholics who have been robbed of a true understanding of Catholic doctrine, which is the saving Truth. A faithful remnant, formed according to what the Church teaches, does remain in North America but, sadly, they are in the minority.

Some time ago, I was preaching in a European country which

used to be one of the great strongholds of Catholicism. At the end of my talk, a man spoke, declaring himself to be a theologian and a priest of a religious order. He was not wearing his habit, which is common among religious in most European countries. He declared that he had heard nothing in my exposition that contradicted the Faith. He believed I was sincere and that nothing I had said bothered him. But then he went on to say that it was like listening to a grandfather of long ago, of the old Church. At the end, he said: "Sin is nothing. God erases it in a second, and that is the line we follow in this group, only God's mercy. Things are no longer the same. We think differently here." I did not want to enter into a debate with him, as I did not think it would help matters. I only asked him how many religious were in his congregation, as I knew that this would be my answer to his speech. He changed his attitude and said: "There are few left in my monastery." I then asked how old they were. He answered: "I'm the youngest." He was sixty-three years of age. For me, that said it all.

The need to exhort the Catholic Church today is no different from the preaching of the apostle, James, to the Romans of Spain in his day. The plain truth can be like vinegar on a wound. There is a great tendency to try to conceal or fabricate the truth, or substitute it with a more palatable, counterfeit that is derived from woolly thinking and clever 'progressive' theology.

These ideas and proposals are so utterly outlandish and yet they are accepted so widely. Sometimes, when I look around, I wonder if the whole world is blind. Is there anyone out there who still lives under the wings of revealed truth? There are some, thank the merciful God. If it was not for this faithful remnant, what would become of us?

The Profession of Faith

What does it mean to profess the faith in the Catholic Church of today?

It is quite common to meet Catholics who are extremely timid about their faith. The more scandals there are, the harder it is for many to remain faithful. We must ask ourselves, 'Is this a proper Christian way of living in our current difficulties and times of trial?' Our Church has even gone through times in which we had two Popes, one false and one true. We have endured many, many battles. Our battle may well be the last, but we cannot say for certain. As the Gospel tells us, "of that day and hour no one knows... but the Father alone." (Matt. 24:36).

If God has decided to cleanse the Church, and to bring to light all that was hidden in the darkness for years, it suggests that an even more profound cleansing is coming upon humanity in general.

Seeing this, I ask myself if it would make any difference if the Catholics who desert the Church, who run away ashamed and scared, were to consider staying to fight for a more obedient and holy clergy. The more I think about it, the more I am inclined to think that it would. We must ensure that all clerical pederasts are brought to justice and hope that this encourages more Catholics to return.

However, we must also understand that some of those who have abandoned the Church should not be there either. God's current *cleansing* also includes their departure. This is a very important moment in time for the Church. God is acting in mysterious and extraordinary ways.

Something very powerful happened at the time of the Reformation in Europe. The number of Catholics who abandoned the Church and invented their own Christianity were replaced by thousands of Mexican Indians who converted to Catholicism through the miracle of Tepeyac; the apparition of Our Lady of Guadalupe to the Indian, Juan Diego.

Also abandoning the Church are a great number of the Irish who are enchanted by the New Age and Christian evangelical sects from America. This is largely due to their disillusionment with the Catholic Church and the scandals of clerical child abuse. At the same time, we see a renewal in the faith of those Irish people who had grown tepid during the economic boom brought by the European Community. Now that the honeymoon with European prosperity seems to be over for Ireland, many who left the Church are returning in the midst of difficult economic conditions.

God is always working, and His perfect plan will be fulfilled despite all our attempts to control the world or to shape it according to our liking. As Catholics, we know that the times in which we are living were clearly announced by Our Lord Jesus Christ. He said: "Watch, therefore, for you do not know when the master of the house will come, in the evening or at midnight, or at cockcrow, or in the morning – lest he come suddenly and find you asleep. And what I say to you I say to all: Watch." (Mark. 13:35-37).

The signs of the times seem so simple and normal, that it is easy to overlook their meaning and importance. It was the same before the Great Flood, the destruction of Sodom and Gomorrah and other world-shaking events. People continued to live a life totally estranged from God, worshipping the material world and its pleasures. Then, all of a sudden, a great change took place which radically transformed their lives overnight.

Today, we see countries with Catholic majorities being governed by atheists who persecute the Church relentlessly. Some of the faithful complain about the injustices they have to endure, but where were these Catholics on voting day when these unjust representatives were being elected? At present, we have seven Communist leaders in Latin America who hate the Catholic Church and who are persecuting Her terribly.

The Lisbon Treaty was approved by countries in the European Union which were once Catholic strongholds. They sold their cultural and Christian identity for benefits that really came down to money in the end.

The battle against abortion has intensified to such an extent that Catholics have finally come to realize just how great a crime it really is. This clearly points to the beginning of a new era of Christianity in which being Christian involves a radical conversion that calls us to the front lines in defense of the Faith. These are no longer the times of a Sunday Mass Catholicism that ends with social pleasantries, coffee and talk of football. Now is the time for planning over that cup of coffee and for hatching plans to protect the Church, and the family, and to defend basic morality and our dearly held values and principles that have been trampled in the filth.

The flags that lesbians and homosexuals fly have been in public squares for years. Their depraved marches have even been arranged outside orphanages where neglected and abandoned children are insinuated into their immoral lifestyle. These movements are part of the seven demonic hierarchies that make up the devil's army.

There will be no peaceful death for those who have failed to ensure the future basis of the Faith for coming generations. We, who are still alive, are called by God to defend the foundations of the Faith that has been entrusted to us.

It is no accident that we are talking about this now and it is certainly not a coincidence that you are reading these lines.

We see how, at the beginning of the Church, the apostles gave their lives for the Lord Jesus, and their blood served as a foundation for many generations, upon which to build their Salvation. In this way, God has provided for the propagation of the Gospel through time. We are all so busy today that we have forgotten our mission and have become players in the infernal drama of our decaying, materialistic culture.

There is talk of a *One-World Government,* of a world without God. There is talk of many things which are clearly not the way for the Eternal Salvation of souls. Satan's whisperings are seducing millions and are being intensely promoted everywhere. Let us turn now to consider the whispering of the Holy Spirit of God, the Kingdom of True Love, the Kingdom of Light.

It is crucial that we understand the Apostles Creed, in the most profound sense of the term. We acknowledge our faith every time we go to Mass on Sundays and, in doing so, we profess that we are of one Church, of one God, of one body, in the communion of saints. We must work in order to be what we profess. We must live what we acknowledge with conviction and courage. In relation to our faith, every step we take in the celebration of the Sacred Liturgy is a specific guideline for what we must do in every aspect of our daily spiritual battle. Our Church is holy and She is the mother of our struggle on earth.

If we acknowledge this, and accept our Catholic Church as the true Mother of our Faith, then we will have a far more profound understanding of our responsibilities. The reason why Catholics give so many scandals to the Church is because they do not know Her, do not love Her, and do not obey or respect Her. They do not understand what She represents and signifies. They do not really know who She is.

It is vitally important for us as Catholics to know the Church well and to defend Her with conviction. We must bring Her to the heart of each person we meet. We represent Her here on earth, we are Her ambassadors and we must behave as such. Wherever we go and whatever we do we are representing our Church, if we are those who sincerely profess the Apostles Creed each Sunday.

One of the most important missions of the *New Evangelization* is to bring back the Baptized. This begins at home. Let us erect fences of wholesome discipline and spiritual attentiveness so that we can protect what is God's, so that we can discover who we are and what our mission is as Catholics in the world today. Life is but a fleeting instant but, in this same instant, many souls are being lost because we are fast asleep and failing in our Christian duty. As Saint Peter, the first Pope reminds us: "Be sober and vigilant. Your opponent the devil is prowling around like a roaring lion looking for someone to devour" (1 Pet. 5:8).

I have met with many different movements within the Catholic Church around the world, both lay and religious. At the beginning of my missionary life, I was impressed by the many charisms we have and the richness of our Church. However, as I traveled more, I observed something that was lacking in the general scheme. People were not working together. There was no mutual support. I was saddened by this discovery. In some ways, we are congregational, like Protestant sects, each one pulling for his own side, without sharing, loving or taking care of the needs of other branches of the same Church. There are some extraordinary exceptions to this, of course, but they are few.

Doubtless, some will not agree with these observations, but I must give testimony to what I have seen, as a lay missionary, and know to be true. My intention in critiquing the state of the Church, as I see it, is not to undermine or discredit Her, but to attempt to waken up the faithful, to encourage them to pull themselves up by their bootstraps and begin to dare to make much needed changes. As Saint Paul urges us: "Encourage yourselves daily while it is still *today*" (Heb. 3:13).

We can see merchants avidly peddling all sorts of ideologies and fables. Their wares can never satisfy the hunger of the masses who only seek to fill their lives with more and more emptiness and confusion. Their hunger is a hunger for death. Their thirst a thirst for darkness.

The unity of the Church is vital for these times and, although it might seem unrealistic at times to even consider it, only Church unity reminds us of Jesus Christ; the only Way, the only Truth and the only Life. In this context, it is right to speak of 'ecumenism' which is the seeking of unity among all Christians.

As I wrote these lines, we were celebrating the first day of the pontificate of our Holy Father, Pope Francis. We certainly cannot read hearts, but we can read signs. The new Pontiff presented these to us from the balcony in Saint Peter's Square, during his first greeting after his election. His were spiritual signs, rich in the poverty of which Jesus speaks in the Gospel.

We are confident that the Holy Spirit has given us a courageous, humble and obedient Pope, who will defend the Church and the whole human family from this culture of death that threatens their destruction. I feel honored to have a Holy Father who speaks my own mother tongue and who is intimately aware of the struggles besetting the Latin American Church. It is truly a sign of great change. We must pray very much for him.

Conclusion

We are one Church, one Body in one God. We must recognize this in our Catholic lives if we are to understand that the need for unity is more burning than ever. If we ignore the call to *New Evangelization*, we will deeply regret it later. The time is ripe to go out and reach all those that have no structure or foundation to their faith; those who participate in the Church like robots, lacking love and understanding of her transcendent greatness, holiness and power.

Great swathes of clerical and religious have become more worldly than godly, and they urgently need to be re-evangelized. We must befriend them and, by the example of our lives, and with much love and charity, help them to turn back to God. By acting now in these particular mission fields within the Church, we have a chance to bring about the change we so greatly need.

Our life is made up of decisions. Whatever we decide, be it good or evil, leaves footprints in eternity. We have been entrusted by God with the future of the Church for those generations yet to come.

We live in a world that tends to intimidate those who are called by God to proclaim the Kingdom. It is important to know that any work of God is going to meet with much opposition and persecution. To be of Christ, and to proclaim His Kingdom among men, means to be crucified with Him. This is the way of the Cross. We must be courageous, prepared to endure the trial, and be humble enough to bend our knees to pray for those who would persecute us. Our battle must be won with the unconditional love that comes only from God. In the end, we will only triumph through love because God is love, and He alone has the victory.

We need to make genuine efforts to love one another with the same love, that Jesus teaches us, in our hearts each day. This is the only way and the only true response if we are to achieve real change and true conversions in the Church. This, in turn, will bring the well-being that families desperately need.

The *New Evangelization* was directed towards Europe at first. Then, a *New Evangelization* was launched from the document of *Aparecida*. Now we realize that Evangelization is truly universal, for the whole Church.

In today's world, there is a crisis in family life. There are a great many dysfunctional families because of the loss of morality and a general lack of the fear of God. We need to work for the healing of the families of the children of light and seek to rescue the families of the children of darkness.

May God have mercy on us all.

***

Heavenly Father, may all the words written in this book glorify you, and may they reach the hearts of each one of the readers to whom You gave the grace to read them; thus, united as one with You, we will be able to contribute abundantly to the economy of salvation, so that Your Son Jesus Christ will return and defeat death forever, and we will be able to live eternally in the Heavenly Jerusalem, together with the whole family of saints whom You have called to Your presence throughout the ages.
Amen.

***

Printed in May 2021
by Rotomail Italia S.p.A., Vignate (MI) - Italy